Air Fryer Cookbook

1000 Day Delicious, Quick & Easy Air Fryer Recipes for Beginners and Advanced Users

By James Walker

Disclaimer and Terms of Use:

Effort has been made to ensure that the information in this book is accurate and complete, however, the author and the publisher do not warrant the accuracy of the information, text and graphics contained within the book due to the rapidly changing nature of science, research, known and unknown facts and internet. The Author and the publisher do not hold any responsibility for errors, omissions or contrary interpretation of the subject matter herein. This book is presented solely for motivational and informational purposes only.

TABLE OF CONTENTS

INTRODUCTION

Welcome to the world of air frying that has been sweeping the nation. As we all know, many individuals love eating deep-fried greasy foods like French fries, fried chicken, and potato chips. Normally, there is a comfort that many of us feel when enjoying a plate of fried food. Apart from the taste, eating fried foods has some benefits. For example, they contain high amounts of calories and fat.

An air fryer is one of the common cooking appliances you will find on the counter space of every kitchen. An air fryer functions just like an oven in the sense that it can roast and bake food. However, the main difference is its heating elements which are located at the top along with a powerful fan that makes foods super crispy in a very short time. Typically, an air fryer heats up superfast, uses less oil, and cooks food evenly in no time. In addition, it is easy to clean an air fryer since most of its racks and baskets are dishwasher safe.

A lot of people choose to use the air fryer to cook packaged frozen foods such as chicken nuggets, tater tots and French fries. Most parents are pleased that their kids can get home from school and safely make something to eat in an air fryer. However, this cooking device can even do more than you think. You can use it to prepare your meals from scratch and even bake items such as burgers, lamb chops, steak and chicken breasts. In addition, you can use an air fryer to cook vegetables in a very short time. A light drizzle of avocado oil or olive oil will make your vegetables to brown and crisp up.

Typically, air frying is seen as a healthy alternative to deep-frying. An air fryer can produce food that is crispy and with crunchy texture on the exterior with just a small amount of oil. This is possible because the air fryers usually transfer heat via convection whereby a large fan circulates hot air and spritz oil droplets all over food. The exposure of food to high temperature and circulation of hot air mimics the outcomes of deep-frying by yielding a crispy browned layer. The convection mechanism means that air fryers just need one tablespoon or so of oil to make foods have a fried-like texture. Since little amount of oil is used, it means that air-fried foods absorb less fat compared to deep-fried counterparts.

WHAT IS AN AIR FRYER?

An air fryer is a cooking device that cooks foods by moving hot air around food using convection mechanism. Basically, this cooking appliance is a smaller version of a convection oven. Hot air is circulated around the food at high speed by a mechanical fan thereby cooking food and yielding a crispy outer layer through the browning reaction of caramelization and Maillard.

Anyone who desires to have the taste and texture of fried food can use the air fryer to achieve that with more convenience than the old-fashioned way of frying food. Generally, air fryers are very easy to use and maintain and hence, owning this appliance is very convenient. Air fryers mostly benefit people who want to eat healthier, love fried food, hate a big clean up after cooking, and want to cook food faster.

If you are looking forward to buying an air fryer from the stores, there are several factors that you need to take into account. Just like any other purchase, knowing the options available in the air fryer is a helpful way in making a good purchasing decision. The majority of air fryers normally use the same basic technology and hence, they have similar features. One thing you should keep in mind is that all the air fryers use a hot air circulation mechanism to cook food and therefore, there is no difference in the designs of air fryers.

Nevertheless, there are several options available for air fryers. Some features you should look into before purchasing include:

- The capacity of the appliance

When buying an air fryer, it is important to know how much foods as well as the types of food you want to cook. Most air fryers usually have the capacity to cook around 1.8 to 2.5 pounds per food. This amount is enough for every day cooking such as drumsticks and fries. Nevertheless, if your main goal is to cook large amount of food such as a whole turkey or chicken, then consider purchasing a larger capacity air fryer.

- Settings and controls

Be sure to check out the settings available on an air fryer and this will help you make a better decision. Most of the air fryers available in the market can reach temperatures of 400 degrees F and some even come with timers to make cooking easy. However, some air fryer models may not get as hot as desired for certain kinds of food you want to cook. It is recommended to check out the maximum temperature the air fryer can reach when cooking food.

In addition, some brands and models of air fryers such as the Philips Viva air fryer come with advanced temperature control settings. You can easily set the temperature you would like the food to cook at by simply choosing anything from 180 F and 400 F.

- Wattage

Since a standard air fryer uses about 800 to 1400 watts, it is important to make sure your kitchen outlets have the capacity to support an air fryer.

HOW DOES THE AIR FRYER WORK?

An air fryer is basically a small convection oven for your kitchen. It is an electric appliance that has a heating element and a strong fan to blow air inside the cooking chamber. The air inside the cooking chamber is usually swirled very fast in a circular motion and in the process it reaches to all the surfaces of food to form a crisp crust. In addition, food is normally placed in a perforated basket to increase its contact with the circulating hot air. The convection effect inside the air fryer cooking chamber ensures that the food cooks and browns on the outside. So long as the temperature of the air reaches around 320 degrees F, breaded foods such as chicken tenders or unbreaded items such as tater tots or French fries will turn brown.

Cooking with an air fryer is very easy and fast. You just need to insert the ingredients into the basket of the air fryer and then set the temperature stated in a recipe. The hot air inside the cooking chamber stimulates a fast flow around the food which results to a cooked inside and a crunchy exterior. Some advanced air fryer models are made with integrated air filters which prevents odors entering inside from the surroundings.

Air fryers solely rely on circulating hot air to cook foods unlike other fryers that require oil to fry foods. This gets rid of the excess fat and oils you would find in foods like chicken nuggets and French fries. There are just a few fryers that can produce fried foods with little or no oil and the air fryer is one of them.

With the mechanism the air fryers use, you can have your desired food prepared within a very short time. For example, you can prepare French fries in about ten to twelve minutes. All air fryers out there have an adjustable timer. This means that once your pre-set time is completed, the air fryer will switch off automatically to keep off the food from overcooking.

The main parts of an air fryer are the basket, pan and air fryer appliance. Apart from those, there are also other items that enhance proper functioning of the fryer. They include baking tin, the divider and double grill layer.

The divider helps you to air fry two ingredients at the same time. In spite of that, if both foods calls for different temperature settings, it's advisable to not to cook both of them at the same time. The baking tin will help you to bake goods such as cookies and cakes in the appliance.

BENEFITS OF USING AN AIR FRYER

There has been an increase in demand for consumption of healthy food all over the world and different sources state that air fryers have helped achieve that. This is because the makers of this kitchen appliance advertise that the device can make fried foods without the adverse health effects of deep-fried foods. Air fried foods are more healthful since they contain less amount of fat than oil-fried foods. However, some individuals are concerned about the health risks that may be associated with this new form of cooking, especially due to fears of cancer and toxicity.

Below are some of the advantages of cooking with an air fryer:

- Time saving

You may want to use an air fryer if you are always on a tight schedule and don't have time to prepare meals. An air fryer can help prepare a snack within a very short while without fuss. The air fryer can be of much help, if your friends come over unexpected and you want to make something by yourself without ordering from the local restaurants.

- Reduces risk of certain diseases

Cooking food in an air fryer can help you avoid trans-fat which are considered harmful processed fats that raise the risk for type 2 diabetes and heart related diseases. The majority of restaurants deep-fry food in trans-fat containing vegetable oils such as canola and research has shown that reusing oil can raise cholesterol and blood pressure leading to vascular inflammation. Replacing deep-frying with air frying can reduce your risk of these complications.

- Reduces the risk of acrylamide formation

Frying your food in oil may lead to development of toxic compounds like acrylamide. This dangerous compound usually forms in certain foods when cooking in high-heat like deep-frying. According to research done by experts, acrylamide have links to the development of certain cancers such as breast, ovarian, oesophageal and pancreatic cancer. In this regard, switching to air frying will lower the risk of developing acrylamide in food.

- Promotes weight loss

High intake of oil-fried foods is directly linked to high risk of obesity since deep-fried foods are well known to contain high amounts of calories and fat. Therefore, switching from oil-fried foods to air fried foods as well as reducing intake of unhealthful oils can promote loss of weight. In addition, air frying requires just a little amount of oil to cook and hence, the total fat content is lower than deep-frying.

WHAT TO EXPECT FROM THIS BOOK

Healthy living is considered a very important thing nowadays and many people are going extra miles to achieve this. For sure, an air fryer usually produces crispy and crunchy food without a single drop of oil. What you might not know is that it also reheats food much better than a microwave. In addition, air frying is the single best way to make breakfast foods, roasted vegetables, and juicy succulent chicken. If you are looking forward to shed some weight and finding it hard to let go of those fatty foods, then replacing deep-fried foods with air fried foods is one of your best solutions. Some of the delicious food around like fried chicken are not good for your overall well-being since they require a lot of oil to cook them. However, you can still enjoy the texture and flavor of oil-fried foods without the negative effects on your well-being with using the air fryer.

This book has a quite large number of awesome recipes that you can try at home if you have plenty of time in the kitchen. Most of the recipes are easy and fast and can be prepared in just a few minutes. In addition, the book has included different types of food groups such as vegetables, milk, poultry, fish, eggs, and grains. Some of the recipes in this book are kid friendly, vegan and others are family friendly.

This air fryer book is divided into the following categories:

1. Breakfast
2. Appetizers
3. Lunch
4. Dinner
5. Seafood
6. Side dishes
7. Snacks
8. Desserts

The recipes in each category mentioned above are simple to prepare and they are well explained. For example, you will find the meal preparation time, cooking time and servings. In addition, the book has easy to understand cooking instructions as well as their nutritional values of each recipe. You will also come across a few cooking tips in some recipes that will be helpful.

From this cookbook you will learn:

1. What is an air fryer?
2. How the air fryers function.
3. The benefits of using an air fryer to cook your food.

This cookbook is a fan favorite among those who love air frying. If you are searching for an ultimate book of air fryer recipes, this one is for you.

MEASUREMENT CONVERSIONS

US Dry Volume Measurements

1/16 teaspoon	Dash
1/8 teaspoon	Pinch
3 teaspoons	1 tablespoon
1/8 cup	2 tablespoons (1 standard coffee scoop)
1/4 cup	4 tablespoons
1/3 cup	5 tablespoons plus 1 teaspoon
1/2 cup	8 tablespoons
3/4 cup	12 tablespoons
1 cup	16 tablespoons
1 pound	16 ounces

US Liquid Volume Measurements

8 Fluid ounces	1 Cup
1 Pint	2 Cups (16 fluid ounces)
1 Quart	2 Pints (4 cups)
1 Gallon	4 Quarts (16 cups)

US to Metric Conversions

1/5 teaspoon	1 ml (ml stands for milliliter, one thousandth of a liter)
1 teaspoon	5 ml
1 tablespoon	15 ml
1 fluid oz.	30 ml
1/5 cup	50 ml
1 cup	240 ml
2 cups (1 pint)	470 ml
4 cups (1 quart)	.95 liter
4 quarts (1 gal)	3.8 liters
1 oz.	28 grams
1 pound	454 grams

Metric to US Conversions

1 milliliter	1/5 teaspoon
5 ml	1 teaspoon
15 ml	1 tablespoon
30 ml	1 fluid oz.
100 ml	3.4 fluid oz.
240 ml	1 cup
1 liter	34 fluid oz.
1 liter	4.2 cups
1 liter	2.1 pints
1 liter	1.06 quarts
1 liter	.26 gallon
1 gram	.035 ounce
100 grams	3.5 ounces
500 grams	1.10 pounds
1 kilogram	2.205 pounds
1 kilogram	35 oz.

Temperature Conversions

Fahrenheit	Celsius	Gas Mark
275° F	140° C	gas mark 1 - cool
300° F	150° C	gas mark 2
325° F	165° C	gas mark 3 - very moderate
350° F	180° C	gas mark 4 - moderate
375° F	190° C	gas mark 5
400° F	200° C	gas mark 6 - moderately hot
425° F	220° C	gas mark 7 - hot
450° F	230° C	gas mark 9
475° F	240° C	gas mark 10 - very hot

Abbreviations:

Cooking Abbreviation(s)	Unit of Measurement
C, c	cup
g	gram
kg	kilogram
L, l	liter
lb	pound
mL, ml	milliliter
oz	ounce
pt	pint
t, tsp	teaspoon
T, TB, Tbl, Tbsp	tablespoon

AIR FRYER RECIPES

BREAKFAST

CRISPY BACON IN THE AIR FRYER

Preparation Time: 10 minutes | Cooking Time: 10 minutes | Servings: 1

Ingredients:

- Bacon – 1 pound

Instructions

1. Place the bacon evenly in your air fryer basket. Depending on the size, it may take two batches to cook all the bacon.
2. Cook bacon for five minutes at 350 degrees F.
3. Flip the bacon and then let to cook for five minutes or until the desired crispiness.
4. Using tongs, remove the bacon and transfer onto a plate lined with paper towel.
5. Cool and then serve.

Nutrition Values:

Calories: 177 | Carbohydrates: 1g | Cholesterol: 37mg | Fat: 13g | Saturated Fat: 5g | Sodium: 637mg | Protein: 13g | Sugar: 0g

Cooking Tip

You may add extra time if necessary since air fryers usually heat differently.

AIR FRIED VEGAN BEIGNETS
WITH AN OVEN OPTION

Preparation Time: 30 minutes | Cooking Time: 6 minutes | Servings: 4

Ingredients:

For dough:

- Unbleached white flour, 3 cups, plus a little more to drizzle onto the chopping board
- Vanilla, 2 teaspoons
- Aquafaba, 2 tablespoons (drained water from can of chickpeas)
- Melted coconut oil

For proofing:

- Active baking yeast, 1 ½ teaspoons
- Powdered baking blend, 3 tablespoons
- Full-fat coconut milk, 1 cup

For powdered baking blend:

- Organic corn starch, 1 teaspoon
- Whole earth sweetener baking blend, 1 cup

Instructions:

1. In a blender, add the cornstarch and whole earth baking blend and then blend till powdery smooth. Cornstarch will prevent it from clumping and hence, you can store the remainder. Alternatively, you can substitute regular powdered sugar later in this recipe.
2. Heat coconut milk till just warm. You should be able to dip your finger without burning yourself. If it is too hot, the yeast will be killed. Pour it into the mixer with the yeast and sugar. Let stand for ten minutes till yeast starts to foam.
3. Stir in the vanilla, aquafaba, and coconut oil with the help of a paddle attachment. Pour in flour, a cup at a time.
4. You can change the dough hook if you already have one, when the flour is mixing in and dough is separating from the sides of the mixer. You can continue using the same paddle if you don't have another.
5. Knead dough in the mixer for around 3 minutes. Dough will probably be wetter than if you were preparing a loaf of bread, although you should be able to scrape it out and form into a ball without it sticking on your hands.
6. Transfer the dough into a mixing bowl, cover using a dish towel and allow to rise for an hour.
7. Drizzle flour onto a large cutting board and then pat the dough out into a rectangle about

1/3 inch thick. Slice into 24 squares and allow to proof for half an hour before cooking them.

8. Preheat an air fryer to 390 F. Place in 3 to 6 beignets at a time depending on the size of the air fryer.

9. Cook on one side for 3 minutes. Turn and cook for 2 more minutes. You may need to cook for 1 or 2 more minutes to get them golden brown depending on your air fryer.

10. Liberally drizzle with powdered baking blend you already made.

11. Continue to cook in batches till all are cooked.

12. Preheat an oven to 350 F. Put beignets in a baking sheet that is covered with parchment paper.

13. Bake them for around 15 minutes or until they are golden brown. Drizzle liberally with the already prepared baking blend.

Nutrition Values:

Calories: 102 | Carbohydrates: 15g | Cholesterol: 0mg | Fat: 3g | Saturated Fat: 3g | Sodium: 2mg | Fiber: 1g | Protein: 3g | Potassium: 3mg | Sugar: 1g

Cooking Tips

You can replace stevia with organic powdered sugar if desired.

AIR FRYER CARROT COFFEE CAKE

Preparation Time: 15 minutes | Cooking Time: 35 minutes | Servings: 6

Ingredients:

- 1/3 cup chopped walnuts, toasted
- 1/4 cup dried cranberries
- 1 cup carrots, shredded
- 1/4 tsp salt
- 1/4 tsp baking soda
- 2 tsp pumpkin pie spice, divided
- 1 tsp baking powder
- 1/3 cup white whole wheat flour
- 2/3 cup all-purpose flour
- 1 tsp vanilla extract
- 1 tsp orange zest, grated
- 2 tbsp. dark brown sugar
- 3 tbsp. canola oil
- 1/3 cup sugar and 2 tbsp. sugar, divided
- 1/2 cup buttermilk
- 1 large egg, lightly beaten, lukewarm

Instructions:

1. Preheat your air fryer to 350 degrees F. Coat a six inch round baking pan with grease and flour. Whisk vanilla, orange zest, brown sugar, oil, 1/3 cup sugar, buttermilk and egg in a large bowl. Whisk baking soda, salt, 1 teaspoon pumpkin pie spice, baking powder and flours in a separate bowl. Slowly beat into the egg mixture. Then fold in dried cranberries and carrots. Transfer to the prepared pan.
2. Combine the remaining one teaspoon of pumpkin spice, remaining two tablespoons of sugar and walnuts in a small bowl. Drizzle evenly onto batter. Carefully put the pan in the air fryer basket.
3. Let to cook for about 35 to 40 minutes until a toothpick comes out clean when inserted in the middle. Cover tightly using foil in case the top becomes too dark. Let cool for ten minutes in the pan placed on a wire rack before you remove from the pan. Serve while warm.

Nutrition Values:

Calories: 316kcal | Carbohydrates: 46g | Cholesterol: 32mg | Fat: 13g | Saturated Fat: 1g | Sodium: 46mg | Fiber: 3g | Protein: 6g | Potassium: 161mg | Sugar: 27g

AIR FRYER EASY EGG CUPS RECIPE

Preparation Time: 10 minutes | Cooking Time: 10 minutes | Servings: 4

Ingredients:

- Egg Beaters 99% egg substitute, ¼ cup, divided
- Shredded Co-Jack cheese, 6 teaspoons, divided
- Frozen chopped spinach, 6 tablespoons, divided
- Sausage, cooked & crumbled, 6 tablespoons, divided

Instructions:

1. Start by cooking the sausage and then set aside.
2. Take the muffin cups and add 1 tablespoon of each sausage crumbles, spinach and 1 teaspoon of cheese. Spread the egg mixture all over the top.
3. Put the muffin cups into the basket and then bake for 10 minutes at 330 F.
4. Let the egg cups to cool a bit before eating.

Nutrition Values:

Calories: 139 | Carbohydrates: 2g | Cholesterol: 20mg | Fat: 12g | Sodium: 249mg | Fiber: 1g | Protein: 6g

AIR FRYER BREAKFAST BISCUIT BOMBS

Preparation Time: 30 minutes | Cooking Time: 15 minutes | Servings: 10

Ingredients:

Biscuit Bombs:

- Sharp Cheddar cheese, 2 oz., chop in 10 half-inch cubes
- Pillsbury Grands Flaky Layers refrigerated biscuits (5 biscuits), 1 can (10.2 oz.)
- Pepper, 1/8 teaspoon
- Salt, 1/8 teaspoon salt
- Eggs, 2 (beaten)
- Bulk breakfast sausage, ¼ lb.
- Vegetable oil, 1 tablespoon

Egg Wash:

- Water - 1 tablespoon
- Egg - 1

Instructions:

1. Start by cutting 2 eight inch rounds of cooking parchment paper. Put one round at the bottom of the air fryer. Spritz with cooking spray.
2. Heat oil over medium-high heat in a ten-inch nonstick skillet. Then cook the sausage in the oil for about 2 to 5 minutes while stirring often to crumble until it is no longer pink. Place in a medium bowl using a slotted spoon. Lower the heat to medium. Add the beaten eggs, pepper and salt to the drippings in the skillet. Let to cook while stirring occasionally until the eggs become thick but still moist. Transfer the eggs to the sausage in the bowl and mix. Let to cool for five minutes.
3. In the meantime, divide the dough into five biscuits and separate each biscuit into two layers. Then press each to form a four-inch round. Pour one heaping tablespoonful of egg mixture on the middle of each round. Place a piece of cheese on top. Fold the edges up gently and over the filling. Pinch to seal. Beat the remaining egg and water in a small bowl. Rub the biscuits on all sides with the egg wash.
4. Put five biscuit bombs onto parchment in the air fryer basket, seam sides down. Use cooking spray to spritz each side of the second parchment round. Place the second parchment round on top of biscuit in the basket. Add the remaining five biscuits on top.
5. Cook for 8 minutes at 325 F. Use tongs to remove the top parchment round. Flip the biscuits carefully and transfer into the basket in a single layer. Let to cook for 4 to 6 more minutes (at least 165 F) or until they are cooked through.

Nutrition Values:

Calories: 190 | Carbohydrates: 13g | Cholesterol: 70mg | Fat: 13g | Saturated Fat: 4 1/2g | Sodium: 420mg | Protein: 7g | Potassium: 50mg | Sugar: 3g

Cooking Tips

You do not have to preheat an air fryer. Just set temperature and start. Do not preheat with parchment paper alone.

Temperature control settings of an air fryer vary depending on the model and brand. If an air fryer doesn't have the exact recommended temperature setting used in the recipe, you should consult the manual for suggested settings.

Do not omit cooking parchment paper. Separating biscuit bombs with parchment keeps them from clumping together.

Make sure the sausage mixture cools for a while before you fill the bombs. This will make dough easier to work with.

AIR FRYER FRITTATA

Preparation Time: 10 minutes | Cooking Time: 10 minutes | Servings: 1

Ingredients:

- Melted Butter, 1 tablespoon
- Cheddar cheese, 2 tablespoons
- Large Eggs, 2
- Chopped Bell Peppers, 1 tablespoon
- Breakfast Sausage Patty, 1
- Chopped Spring Onions, 1 tablespoon
- Pepper and salt to taste

Instructions:

1. Brush a mini loaf pan or a four inch cake pan generously with butter.
2. In the greased pan, put sliced up breakfast sausage and then air fry for 5 minutes at 350 F.
3. In the meantime, crack two eggs in a medium bowl. Season with pepper and salt and then whisk thoroughly.
4. Pour in the chopped bell peppers and spring onion. Combine well. When sausage is cooked through, pour in egg mixture. Combine well with sausages.
5. Drizzle cheddar cheese on top and then air fry for five minutes at 350 F.
6. Serve hot along with fresh tomato salsa.

Nutrition Values:

Calories: 400 | Carbohydrates: 3g | Cholesterol: 441mg | Fat: 34g | Saturated Fat: 16g | Sodium: 850mg | Protein: 21g | Sugar: 1g

Cooking Tips

You can use shredded chicken, ham or bacon in place of breakfast sausage.

Replace bell peppers and spring onion with your favorite vegetable combination such as broccoli, tomatoes, and spinach.

AIR-FRIED BREAKFAST BOMBS ARE A PORTABLE HEALTHY MEAL

Preparation Time: 10 minutes | Cooking Time: 16 minutes | Servings: 2

Ingredients:

- 4 ounces whole-wheat pizza dough, freshly prepared
- 1 tablespoon fresh chives, chopped
- 1 ounce 1/3-less-fat cream cheese, softened
- 3 large eggs, lightly beaten
- 3 center-cut bacon pieces

Instructions:

1. In a medium skillet, cook bacon over medium heat, about ten minutes, till very crispy. Transfer bacon from pan and crumble. Add the eggs to the bacon drippings in the pan. Cook while stirring frequently, about one minute until nearly set but still loose. Place the eggs in a bowl and stir in crumbled bacon, chives, and cream cheese.
2. Separate the dough into four pieces of equal size. Then on a lightly floured surface, roll each piece into a five inch circle. Smear the outside edge of the dough with water. Then wrap the dough around the egg mixture to make a purse and pinch the dough at the seams.
3. Put the dough purses in an air fryer basket in a single layer. Spray well cooking spray. Let to cook for 5 to 6 minutes at 350 F till golden brown, checking after four minutes.

Nutrition Values:

Calories: 305 | Carbohydrates: 26g | Fat: 15g | Saturated Fat: 5g | Sodium: 548mg | Fiber: 2g | Protein: 19g | Sugars: 1g

AIR FRYER BACON AND EGG BREAKFAST BISCUIT BOMBS

Preparation Time: 35 minutes | Cooking Time: 15 minutes | Servings: 8

Ingredients:

Egg wash

- Water - 1 tablespoon
- Egg - 1

Biscuit Bombs

- Sharp cheddar cheese - 2 oz., (chopped into ten 3/4-inch cubes)
- Pillsbury Grands Southern Homestyle refrigerated Buttermilk biscuits (five biscuits) - 1 can (10.2 oz.)
- Pepper - ¼ teaspoon
- Beaten eggs - 2
- Butter 1 tablespoon
- Bacon - 4 slices (chopped into 1/2-inch pieces)

Instructions:

1. Cut 2 eight inch rounds cooking parchment paper. Put one round at the bottom of an air fryer basket. Spritz with cooking spray.
2. Cook bacon in a ten inch nonstick skillet over medium-high heat till crisp. Transfer from pan to paper towel. Gently wipe the skillet with paper towel. Place in butter and melt over medium heat. Pour two beaten eggs and pepper into the skillet. Let to cook while stirring often until the eggs become thickened but still moist. Transfer from heat and mix in bacon. Let to cool for five minutes.
3. In the meantime, divide the dough into five biscuits and then separate each biscuit into two layers. Press each to form a four inch round. Pour one heaping tablespoon of egg mixture onto the middle of each round. Place a piece of cheese on top. Carefully fold the edges up and over the filling. Pinch together to seal. Beat water and remaining egg in a small bowl. Rub the biscuits on all sides with the egg wash.
4. Put five of biscuits on the parchment in the air fryer basket, seam sides down. Spritz each side of the second parchment round with cooking spray. Place the second parchment round on top of the bombs in basket. Add the remaining five bombs on top.
5. Cook at 325 F for 8 minutes. Use tongs to remove the top parchment round. Gently flip the biscuits and transfer into basket in a single layer. Let to cook for about 4 to 6 minutes (at least 165 F) or till they're cooked through.

Nutrition Values:

Calories: 200 | Carbohydrates: 17g | Cholesterol: 85mg | Fat: 12g | Saturated Fat: 6g | Sodium: 440mg | Protein: 7g | Potassium: 50mg | Sugar: 3g

AIR-FRIED CINNAMON AND SUGAR DOUGHNUTS

Preparation Time: 25 minutes | Cooking Time: 16 minutes | Servings: 9

Ingredients:

- Melted butter, 2 tablespoons or as desired
- Cinnamon, 1 teaspoon
- White sugar, ⅓ cup
- Sour cream, ½ cup
- Salt, 1 teaspoon
- Baking powder, 1 ½ teaspoons
- All-purpose flour, 2 ¼ cups
- 2 large egg yolks
- Butter at lukewarm, 2 ½ tablespoons
- White sugar, ½ cup

Instructions:

1. In a bowl, mix butter and ½ cup of white sugar together until crumbly. Stir in the egg yolks until combined well.
2. In a separate bowl, sift salt, baking powder and flour. Pour half the sour cream and 1/3 of flour mixture into the sugar-egg mixture. Then stir till combined. Mix in the remaining sour cream and flour. Place the dough to the refrigerator until when ready to use.
3. In a bowl, combine together cinnamon and 1/3 cup of sugar.
4. On a lightly floured surface, roll out the dough to half inch thick. Slice nine large circles in the dough and then make a small circle out of the middle of each large circle to form doughnut shapes.
5. Preheat the air fryer to 350 F.
6. Brush half of melted butter onto each side of the doughnut.
7. Transfer half doughnuts into the basket of your air fryer and then cook for 8 minutes. Rub the cooked doughnuts with the remaining butter and then immediately dunk into the sugar-cinnamon mixture. Repeat the steps with the remaining doughnuts.

Nutrition Values:

Calories: 276 | Carbohydrates: 43.5g | Cholesterol: 66mg | Fat: 9.7g | Sodium: 390mg | Fiber: 1g | Protein: 4.3g | Potassium: 59mg | Sugar: 19g

AIR FRYER BREAKFAST TOAD-IN-THE-HOLE TARTS

Preparation Time: 5 minutes | Cooking Time: 25 minutes | Servings: 4

Ingredients:

- Eggs - 4
- Diced cooked ham - 4 tablespoons
- Chopped fresh chives, if desired
- Shredded Cheddar cheese - 4 tablespoons
- Frozen puff pastry (thawed) - 1 sheet

Instructions:

1. Start by preheating your air fryer to 400 F.
2. Then unfold the pastry sheet onto a flat surface and slice into four squares.
3. Transfer the pastry squares into the basket of the air fryer and let to cook for about 6 to 8 minutes.
4. Remove the basket from the air fryer. Gently press each square to make an indentation with a metal tablespoon. Put 1 tablespoon of ham and 1 tablespoon cheddar cheese in each hole. Then add one egg on top of each.
5. Place basket back into the air fryer. Cook for around six minutes to the desired doneness. Transfer tarts from the basket and cool for five minutes. Repeat with the rest of pastry squares, eggs, ham and cheese.
6. Decorate tarts with chives if desired.

Nutrition Values:

Calories: 446 | Carbohydrates: 27.9 g | Cholesterol: 199 mg | Fat: 31 g | Saturated Fat: 9.2 g | Sodium: 377 mg | Protein: 14.2 g | Potassium: 137 mg | Sugar: 1 g

Cooking Tip

The simplest way add the egg into the hole is to first crack it into a small glass and then pour in the hole.

LUNCH

AIR-FRIED FALAFEL

Preparation Time: 20 minutes | Cooking Time: 15 minutes | Servings: 4

Ingredients:

- 1 1/2 tsp. sea salt
- 1/2 tsp. cayenne pepper
- 1 tsp. ground black pepper
- 2 tsp. ground coriander
- 2 tsp. cumin powder
- 1 Tbsp. chickpea flour
- 1/4 cup chopped cilantro leaves
- 3/4 cup chopped flat-leaf parsley leaves
- 2 cloves minced garlic
- 1 diced onion
- 2 cups dried chickpeas (soaked)

Instructions:

1. Put all ingredients in a food processor and then pulse till chickpeas are minced finely. Don't over-pulse. The mixture should be coarse and not pasty or smooth.
2. Use hands to form the mixture into small balls of about 1.5-inch in diameter. Place about nine balls in the air fryer basket in a single layer. Then air fry at 370 to 380 F for about 15 minutes. Repeat until all dough is used up. Falafel balls are done when they're crisp and golden brown.
3. If you do not have an air fryer, bake falafel for about half an hour at 375 F until golden brown, turning once when halfway for even cooking. In addition, you can pan-fry falafel in small amount of olive oil over medium heat till browned evenly.
4. You can store any leftover falafel while covered in a fridge for a few days but they're best served fresh. Reheat in an air fryer or oven at 325 F.
5. To extend the shelf life, put uncooked falafel in a cookie sheet. Then place the cookie sheet in your freezer for about one hour. Remove sheet from freezer and transfer falafel balls to a container or freezer-safe bag. Return them into freezer. To thaw, transfer the uncooked falafel to a fridge one day before you cook.

Nutrition Values:

Calories: 56 | Carbohydrates: 9 g | Fat: 1 g | Fiber: 5 g | Protein: 3 g | Sugar: 2 g

Cooking Tips

You can soften up the chickpeas by soaking in water for twenty-four hours. Once soaked, drain off water and rinse chickpeas well. Don't cook them.

Two cups of dried chickpeas can yield approximately five cups of soaked chickpeas.

Note that the preparation time doesn't include soaking chickpeas.

AIR FRYER TOFU BUDDHA BOWL

Preparation Time: 15 minutes | Cooking Time: 35 minutes | Servings: 6

Ingredients:

- 2 cups cooked brown rice or quinoa
- 8 oz. fresh spinach sautéed with garlic and olive oil
- 1 thinly chopped red bell pepper
- 3 medium carrots, peeled and thinly chopped
- 1 lb. fresh broccoli florets only
- 1 Tbsp. Sriracha
- 2 Tbsp. lime juice
- 3 Tbsp. molasses
- 1/4 cup soy sauce
- 2 Tbsp. sesame oil
- 14 oz. extra firm tofu

Instructions:

1. Wrap the tofu with several paper towels and then place a plate on top to squeeze out the excess liquid. Unwrap tofu when dry and chop it into tiny cubes (around 100 pieces).
2. In a large bowl, add sriracha, lime juice, molasses, soy sauce and sesame oil. Then whisk until well incorporated.
3. Transfer tofu to the sauce and allow it to marinate for about 5 to 10 minutes, stirring frequently. As the tofu marinates, prepare the vegetables.
4. Brush an air fryer with your favorite oil. Transfer the tofu from the bowl to an air fryer basket and leave the marinade in the bowl. Cook the tofu for 15 minutes at 370 F, shaking the basket after every five minutes.
5. In the meantime, add bell pepper, carrots and broccoli to the bowl with the marinade and combine thoroughly every few minutes.
6. In addition, as the tofu cooks, cook the spinach over the stovetop until just wilted. Do not overcook it.
7. Remove tofu from the air fryer once done and set aside. Place the veggies into the air fryer basket leaving the marinade in the bowl. Cook the veggies for ten minutes shaking the basket well after every few minutes.
8. Start building your Buddha bowl in large serving bowl. Pour in cooked rice or quinoa, and then evenly spread the cooked veggies. Add cooked spinach and lastly add tofu. Top with the remaining marinade and decorate with sesame seeds.

Nutrition Values:

Calories: 236kcal | Carbohydrates: 31g | Fat: 8g | Saturated Fat: 1g | Sodium: 731mg | Fiber: 6g | Protein: 12g | Potassium: 926mg | Sugar: 11g

AIR FRYER CRAB FRIED RICE

Preparation Time: 10 minutes | Cooking Time: 20 minutes | Servings: 5

Ingredients:

- Red pepper flakes – 1 tbsp. (optional)
- Cilantro (optional)
- Pepper and salt
- Chili powder – 1 tsp. (optional)
- Paprika – 1 tsp.
- Sesame oil – 1 tsp.
- Sesame oil – 1 tbsp. (Feel free to use hot chili sesame oil)
- Fish sauce – 1 tbsp.
- Low sodium soy sauce – 3 tbsp.
- Chopped green onions – 2
- Minced garlic cloves – 3 to 4
- Chopped red onion – ½
- Ready rice brown rice – 2 packets
- Scrambled and cooked medium eggs – 2
- Lump crab meat – 6 oz.

Instructions:

1. Cook the rice and then put in your fridge. You will need to cool the rice for about 15 to 20 minutes. Feel free to put it in your freezer till cold.
2. Pour one teaspoon sesame oil onto the bottom of push pan.
3. In a large bowl, mix red pepper flakes, green onions, red onions, garlic and cold rice. Sprinkle remaining sesame oil all over top and stir.
4. Pour the mixture into push pan and then put the pan into an air fryer.
5. Set the air fryer to 375 F and let to cook for 15 minutes.
6. Season crab with pepper, salt, chili powder, and paprika.
7. Remove push pan and then add soy sauce, fish sauce, and crab to rice. Combine thoroughly.
8. Continue to cook for five more minutes.
9. Remove rice from air fryer and stir in scrambled eggs. Drizzle cilantro on top.
10. Let to cool and then serve.

Nutrition Values:

Calories: 268kcal | Carbohydrates: 31g | Fat: 11g | Saturated Fat: g | Protein: 15g

Cooking Tips

The cooking time may vary depending on your air fryer. Be sure to look at the color of the rice. It's done when dark brown in color and after reaching your preferred crunchiness.

You can use more or less soy sauce as you like.

For extra flavor, add lime juice or fresh squeezed lemon.

AIR FRYER DRY RUB CHICKEN WINGS

Preparation Time: 30 minutes | Cooking Time: 12 minutes | Servings: 4

Ingredients:

- Cayenne Pepper - 1 Tbsp.
- Black Pepper - 1 Tbsp.
- White Pepper - 1 Tbsp.
- Thyme - 1 Tbsp.
- Onion - 1 Tbsp.
- Garlic - 1 Tbsp.
- Oregano - 1 Tbsp.
- Basil - 1 Tbsp.
- White sugar - 2 Tbsp.
- Paprika - 2 Tbsp.
- Chicken Wings - 1 lb. (fresh or frozen then thaw)

Instructions:

1. Begin by preheating an air fryer to 400 F for four to five minutes.
2. In a bowl, add sugar and spices together.
3. Combine thoroughly.
4. Dunk each chicken wing into the mix and rub each side of the wings.
5. Put the chicken in a bowl and marinate for 30 to 45 minutes.
6. Spread the chicken in your air fryer in a single layer.
7. Cook for 12 minutes at 400 F.
8. Turn the wings when halfway cooking to ensure even cooking.

Nutrition Values:

Calories: 306 | Carbohydrates: 12g | Cholesterol: 87mg | Fat: 18g | Saturated Fat: 5g | Sodium: 86mg | Fiber: 3g | Protein: 22g | Potassium: 327mg | Sugar: 6g

AIR FRYER ROAST BEEF

Preparation Time: 5 minutes | Cooking Time: 45 minutes | Servings: 6

Ingredients:

- 2 tsp rosemary and thyme (dried or fresh)
- 1 tsp salt
- 1 medium onion (if desired)
- 1 tbsp. olive oil
- 2 lb. beef roast

Instructions:

1. Preheat your air fryer to 390 degrees F.
2. Combine oil, rosemary and sea salt on a plate.
3. Pat dry beef roast with paper towels. Put the beef on the plate and flip to coat it with the oil-herb mix.
4. Transfer the beef roast to an air fryer basket.
5. Peel the onion if using and slice in half. Put onion halves close to the beef roast in the basket.
6. Cook for fifteen minutes.
7. Once time is done, lower the temperature to 360 F. You may need to turn the food when cooking in some air fryers and hence, it's advisable to consult your manual and flip the beef if necessary.
8. Cook the roast beef for 30 more minutes. It should be medium-rare. It's recommended to use a meat thermometer to check the beef's temperature to ensure it's cooked as desired. You can cook for extra five minutes intervals if you like the meat more well done.
9. Remove the meat from air fryer, encase with foil and let to sit for at least 10 minutes prior to serving. This enables the beef to finish cooking and reabsorption of the juices into the meat.
10. Thinly slice the beef against the grain and then serve with steamed or roasted veggies, gravy and wholegrain mustard.

Nutrition Values:

Calories: 212kcal | Carbohydrates: 2g | Cholesterol: 83mg | Fat: 7g | Saturated Fat: 2g | Sodium: 282mg | Fiber: 1g | Protein: 33g | Potassium: 536mg | Sugar: 1g

AIR FRYER ROAST PORK

Preparation Time: 5 minutes | Cooking Time: 50 minutes | Servings: 6

Ingredients:

- 1 tablespoon salt
- 1 tablespoon olive oil
- 2 lb. pork loin

Instructions:

1. Preheat your air fryer to 360 F.
2. If pork has rind, slice the skin using a knife and be sure that it has got deep scores right through.
3. Sprinkle oil onto the pork and then rub into skin. Drizzle salt on top of skin and rub it in.
4. Cook the pork for 50 minutes in the air fryer (25 minutes per pound of meat).
5. To know whether the meat is done, insert a knife at the thickest part; the meat is cooked if the juices run clear. Alternatively, you can use a meat thermometer to check when done. It's done when the temperature reaches 145 degrees F.
6. Remove pork from your air fryer, cover with foil and let to sit for 10 minutes prior to serving. If cracking isn't as crisp as desired at this point, remove it before you rest the pork and return to the air fryer for 10 minutes.

Nutrition Values:

Calories: 220kcal | Cholesterol: 95mg | Fat: 8g | Saturated Fat: 2g | Sodium: 849mg | Protein: 33g | Potassium: 565mg

AIR FRYER ROAST LAMB

Preparation Time: 5 minutes | Cooking Time: 15 minutes | Servings: 2

Ingredients:

- Black pepper - 1/2 tsp
- Thyme (fresh or dried) - 1 tsp
- Rosemary (fresh or dried) - 1 tsp
- Olive oil - 1 tbsp.
- Butterflied lamb leg roast - 10 oz.

Instructions:

1. Preheat your air fryer to 360 degrees F.
2. Combine one tablespoon olive oil with one teaspoon each of thyme and rosemary on a plate.
3. Pat dry the lamb and put it on the herb-oil mixture. Flip the meat to coat it well.
4. Transfer the lamb to the air fryer and then cook for 15 minutes.
5. It should be medium-rare. It's best to use a meat thermometer to check the temperature of the lamb to ensure it's cooked as desired. The temperature reach 140 to 150 degrees F for medium-rare. To have it more done, you can cook for extra three minutes intervals.
6. Transfer the lamb from the air fryer, cover with foil and then let to sit for 5 minutes prior to serving.
7. Slice against the grain and serve.

Nutrition Values:

Calories: 181 | Carbohydrates: 1g | Cholesterol: 57mg | Fat: 11g | Saturated Fat: 2g | Sodium: 56mg | Protein: 18g | Potassium: 258mg

AIR FRYER TURKEY BREAST

Preparation Time: 5 minutes | Cooking Time: 50 minutes | Servings: 4

Ingredients:

- Minced garlic - 2 tbsp.
- Rosemary and thyme - 2 tsp
- Olive oil - 3 tbsp.
- 1 turkey half-breast (about 2lb or 1kg)

Instructions:

1. Preheat an air fryer to 360 degrees F.
2. On a plate combine garlic, herbs and oil. Put the turkey on the herb mixture and flip to coat it well.
3. Transfer the turkey to your air fryer basket, skin side down. Cook for 20 minutes.
4. Remove basket from air fryer and flip the turkey over.
5. Place back the meat into your air fryer and cook for 30 minutes.
6. The meat is done when its juices run clear after inserting a knife into the thickest part. To be sure it's cooked, the internal temperature should reach 165 degrees F when measured with a meat thermometer. Cook for extra ten minute intervals in case the turkey needs more cooking.
7. Let to sit for at least ten minutes while covered before you serve.

Nutrition Values:

Calories: 231 | Cholesterol: 84mg | Fat: 10g | Saturated Fat: 1g | Sodium: 321mg | Protein: 33g | Potassium: 377mg

AIR FRYER PORK CHOPS

Preparation Time: 1 minute | Cooking Time: 12 minutes | Servings: 1

Ingredients:

- 1/2 teaspoon seasoning
- 1 pork chop (about 4 oz.)

Instructions:

1. Preheat your air fryer to 360 degrees F.
2. Pat dry the pork and then season with pepper and salt or your preferred seasoning.
3. Transfer the meat to an air fryer basket. Do not overlap the chops if cooking more than one.
4. Let to cook for 12 minutes until golden brown. You can check the internal temperature with a meat thermometer if unsure when done. It should reach 145 degrees F when done.

Nutrition Values:

Calories: 214kcal | Carbohydrates: 1g | Cholesterol: 89mg | Fat: 9g | Saturated Fat: 3g | Sodium: 64mg | Protein: 29g | Potassium: 499mg

APPETIZERS

AIR FRYER BOW TIE PASTA CHIPS

Preparation Time: 30 minutes | Cooking Time: 10 minutes | Servings: 2

Ingredients:

- 1/2 teaspoon salt
- 1 1/2 teaspoon (3 g) Italian Seasoning Blend
- 1 tablespoon (7 g) nutritional yeast
- 1 tablespoon (15 ml) olive oil (you can use aquafaba)
- 2 cups (152 g) dry whole wheat bow tie pasta (make it gluten-free by using brown rice pasta)

Instructions:

1. Start by cooking pasta for half the time indicated on the package. Then drain and toss the pasta with the nutritional yeast, salt, Italian seasoning and aquafaba or olive oil.
2. If the air fryer basket is small, add about ½ of the mixture. If large enough, you can cook in one batch.
3. Set to cook for 5 minutes at 390 degrees F. Then shake the air fryer basket and let to cook for about 3-5 minutes or till crunchy. The chips will crisp up more when cooling.

Nutrition Values:

Calories: 294kcal | Carbohydrates: 49g | Fat: 8g | Saturated Fat: 1g | Sodium: 587mg | Fiber: 2g | Protein: 10g | Potassium: 250mg

AIR FRYER MUSHROOM ROLL-UPS

Preparation Time: 30 minutes | Cooking Time: 10 minutes | Servings: 10

Ingredients:

- Chutney
- Cooking spray
- 10 (8 inches) flour tortillas
- 4 ounces whole-milk ricotta cheese
- 1 package (8 ounces) softened cream cheese
- 1/4 tsp salt
- 1/2 tsp red pepper flakes, crushed
- 1 tsp thyme, dried
- 1 tsp oregano, dried
- 8 ounces large finely chopped Portobello mushrooms, gills removed
- 2 tbsp. extra virgin olive oil

Instructions:

1. Heat oil in your skillet on medium heat. Place in the mushrooms and then sauté for four minutes. Add salt, pepper flakes, thyme and oregano. Sauté for about 4 to 6 minutes until the mushrooms become browned. Let to cool.
2. Mix the cheeses and then fold in the mushrooms, stirring well. Pour three tablespoons of the mushroom mixture at the bottom-center of each tortilla. Then roll up tightly and hold in place with toothpicks.
3. Preheat your air fryer to 400 degrees F. Put the roll-up into greased tray in the basket of air fryer, in batches. Spray with cooking spray. Let to cook for about 9 to 11 minutes until turned golden brown. Once the roll-ups cool enough to handle, get rid of the toothpicks. You can serve together with chutney.

Nutrition Values:

Calories: 291 | Carbohydrates: 31g | Cholesterol: 27mg | Fat: 16g | Saturated Fat: 7g | Sodium: 380mg | Fiber: 2g | Protein: 8g | Potassium: mg | Sugar: 2g

CRISPY BRUSSELS SPROUTS – AIR FRYER

Preparation Time: 5 minutes | Cooking Time: 12 minutes | Servings: 2

Ingredients:

- Garlic powder – ½ teaspoon (if you like)
- Black pepper – ¼ teaspoon
- Salt – ½ teaspoon
- Olive oil – 1 tablespoon
- Brussels sprouts – 10 (approx. ½ lb.)

Instructions:

1. Wash the Brussels sprouts with water and then pat dry with paper towel.
2. Slice the bottom stem and then slice each sprout in half. Transfer to a bowl.
3. Toss Brussels sprouts with garlic powder, pepper, salt and olive oil. Then place then into an air fryer basket.
4. Cook for 12 minutes in the air fryer at 360 degrees F or until browned slightly. Be sure to shake when halfway through.
5. Transfer Brussels sprouts onto a serving plate and sprinkle lime juice on top. Enjoy them alone or with a dip of garlic thyme mayonnaise.

Nutrition Values:

Calories: 104kcal | Carbohydrates: 9.31g | Fat: 7.05g | Saturated Fat: 0.998g | Sodium: 606mg | Fiber: 3.8g| Protein: 3.38g | Potassium: 384mg | Sugar: 2.11g

Cooking Tips

For variations:

Add breadcrumbs and parmesan along with olive oil before you cook.

You can toss Brussels sprouts in buffalo sauce.

VEGAN FRIED RAVIOLI IN THE AIR FRYER

Preparation Time: 15 minutes | Cooking Time: 8 minutes | Servings: 4

Ingredients:

- 1/2 cup marinara (for dipping)
- Spritz cooking spray
- 8 ounces vegan ravioli (frozen or thawed)
- 1/4 cup aquafaba (liquid from a can of chickpeas or other beans)
- Salt and pepper
- 1 tsp garlic powder
- 1 tsp dried oregano
- 1 tsp dried basil
- 2 tsp nutritional yeast flakes
- 1/2 cup panko bread crumbs

Instructions:

1. Mix nutritional yeast flakes, panko bread crumbs, garlic powder, dried oregano, dried basil, pepper and salt on a plate.
2. In a separate small bowl, place aquafaba.
3. Dunk the ravioli into aquafaba, shake to get rid of excess liquid and then dredge it in the bread crumb mixture. Ensure the ravioli is covered fully. Place ravioli in your air fryer basket and do not overlap them to ensure even browning. You can air fry in batches if necessary.
4. Spray ravioli with cooking spray.
5. Cook for 6 minutes at 390 F. Gently turn each ravioli over and continue to cook for two minutes. (Avoid shaking the basket since you could lose lots of bread crumbs).
6. Transfer ravioli from air fryer. Serve along with warm marinara.

Nutrition Values:

Calories: 150kcal | Carbohydrates: 27g | Sodium: 411mg Fiber: 2g | Protein: 5g | Potassium: 145mg | Sugar: 1g

Cooking Tips

You can use frozen or thawed ravioli in this recipe. Frozen ravioli are usually stuck together and hence, you should thaw them in a fridge to separate them.

It most cases there will be leftover panko bread crumb mixture in this recipe. Place it in a plastic bag and store in your fridge for future use.

Feel free to use cooking liquid from beans if cooking beans from scratch. You can also use vegan mayonnaise if it's hard to get aquafaba. Make sure to wipe off the excess mayo. Furthermore, you can still use non-dairy milk combined with a spoonful of cornstarch.

AIR FRYER CHICKEN WINGS

Preparation Time: 5 minutes | Cooking Time: 30 minutes | Servings: 4

Ingredients:

- 2 lb. chicken wings (slice into drumettes and flats)

For buffalo chicken wing sauce (if desired)

- 1/4 cup Frank's RedHot Original Cayenne Pepper Sauce
- 1/4 cup butter, unsalted

Instructions:

1. Preheat the air fryer as directed on the manual. Put the chicken into a basket and place it in the air fryer.
2. Set to cook at 380 degrees F for 24 minutes, shaking basket after every ten minutes to evenly cook.
3. Once time is done, shake the air fryer basket and change the temperature to 400 degrees F. Cook for six minutes or till the skin is crispy and golden brown. You can cook the wings in batches depending on the size of the air fryer.
4. Place the chicken in a bowl and then toss with buffalo wing sauce or your favorite BBQ.

To prepare buffalo sauce (if desired)

1. In a bowl, whisk together hot sauce and melted.

Nutrition Values:

Calories: 272kcal | Cholesterol: 94mg | Fat: 20g | Saturated Fat: 5g | Sodium: 89mg | Protein: 22g | Potassium: 191mg

IFTEEN MINUTE AIR FRYER THREE CHEESE STUFFED MUSHROOMS

Preparation Time: 7 minutes | Cooking Time: 8 minutes | Servings: 5

Ingredients:

- 2 chopped garlic cloves
- 1 tsp Worcestershire sauce
- 1/8 cup shredded white cheddar cheese
- 1/8 cup shredded sharp cheddar cheese
- ¼ cup parmesan cheese shredded
- 4 oz. cream cheese (Use reduced-fat)
- Salt and pepper
- 8 oz. large fresh mushrooms (use Monterey)

Instructions:

1. Take the mushroom and cut the stem out to prepare it for stuffing. You can slice off the stem first and then slice a circular cut where the stem was. Keep cutting till you get rid of the excess mushroom.
2. Put cream cheese in your microwave and heat for 15 seconds to soften it.
3. In a medium bowl, mix the Worcestershire sauce, pepper, salt, all the shredded cheeses and cream cheese.
4. Fill mushrooms with the cheese mixture.
5. Transfer mushrooms in your air fryer and cook for 8 minutes at 370 F.
6. Cool the mushrooms before you serve.

Nutrition Values:

Calories: 116kcal | Carbohydrates: 3g | Fat: 8g | Protein: 8g

AIR FRYER MOZZARELLA STICKS

Preparation Time: 20 minutes | Cooking Time: 5 minutes | Servings: 4

Ingredients:

- 1/2 - 1 tsp smoked paprika
- 1/2 - 1 tsp salt
- 1/2 - 1 tsp onion powder
- 1/2 - 1 tsp chili powder
- 1/2 - 1 tsp garlic powder
- 1/4 cup panko
- 1 large egg
- 1 (10 oz.) package part skim mozzarella string cheese (each stick sliced in half)
- 1/4 cup breadcrumbs
- 1/4 cup whole wheat flour
- Ranch (for dipping)
- Marinara sauce (for dipping)

Instructions:

1. Put the halved cheese sticks in a zip lock bag and put in your freezer for at least half an hour until frozen.
2. Whisk the egg in a shallow bowl until broken up. Keep it aside.
3. In another shallow bowl, put smoked paprika, chili powder, salt, garlic powder, onion powder, panko and breadcrumbs. Then whisk till combined and set aside.
4. Line parchment paper or silicon mat onto a rimmed baking sheet.
5. Put flour and frozen cheese sticks in another zip lock bag and then shake till cheese sticks are well coated with flour.
6. Get rid of the excess flour.
7. Dip one cheese stick in the egg till well coated and then dip in panko mixture till coated well.
8. Transfer onto the lined baking sheet. Repeat this process with the remaining cheese sticks.
9. Transfer the baking sheet to your freezer for at least 1 hour until the cheese sticks are frozen.
10. Switch your air fryer on.
11. Press the preheat button, then set temperature to 370 F and the timer to 5 minutes.
12. Press start.
13. Once preheating is complete, the air fryer will beep.
14. Spritz the air fryer basket with cooking spray.
15. Put the mozzarella sticks in the basket and do not overcrowd. You can work with about six at a time.
16. Close your air fryer and let to cook. You should hear a beep sound once done.
17. Repeat with the remaining mozzarella sticks. Keep the uncooked leftovers in your freezer.
18. Serve along with dipping sauces.

Nutrition Values:

Calories: 48kcal | Carbohydrates: 2g | Cholesterol: 13mg | Fat: 2g | Saturated Fat: 1g | Sodium: 206mg | Protein: 3g | Potassium: 14mg

Cooking Tips

For a little more aggressively seasoned stick, you can add one teaspoon of each spice.

You can make these in advance after mozzarella sticks are frozen in baking sheet. Just place them in a zip lock bag and then store in your freezer for about two to three months.

AIR FRYER RAVIOLI

Preparation Time: 10 minutes | Cooking Time: 12 minutes | Servings: 6

Ingredients:

For ravioli:

- 1 cup warmed marinara sauce (for dipping)
- 1/2 bag mini cheese ravioli, store-bought (around 18-20 ravioli)
- 1 large egg
- non-stick canola cooking spray (if desired)

For dredge:

- 1 tsp Italian seasoning
- 1/4 cup Parmesan, freshly grated
- 1 cup Panko bread crumbs

Optional garnishes:

- 2 tbsp. grated parmesan cheese

Instructions:

1. Prepare a dredge area with 2 bowls. Beat the egg in the first bowl. Mix all of the dredge ingredients in the second bowl.
2. Prepare ravioli. Keep ravioli frozen till when ready to dredge. Dunk ravioli into the beaten egg, then dredge into the breadcrumbs and place in an air fryer basket.
3. Repeat this process with the remaining ravioli.
4. Spritz ravioli with non-stick cooking spray if desired to facilitate even browning. Close your air fryer and hit the power button. Push the "m" button and then select "Fly". Change the temperature to 400 F and set timer to 12 minutes. Shake the basket when halfway through and flip ravioli over. If necessary, add more cooking spray.
5. Decorate with more parmesan cheese and then serve hot with marinara sauce.

Nutrition Values:

Calories: 107 | Carbohydrates: 12g | Cholesterol: 35mg | Fat: 3g | Saturated Fat: 1g | Sodium: 434mg | Protein: 5g | Potassium: 164mg | Sugar: 2g

AIR FRYER TOFU

Preparation Time: 5 minutes | Cooking Time: 15 minutes | Servings: 2

Ingredients:

- olive oil
- ½ teaspoon salt
- ½ teaspoon brown sugar
- 1 teaspoon flour
- 2 teaspoon five spice
- 10 oz. tofu (firm style)

Instructions:

1. Preheat your air fryer to 360 degrees F.
2. In a bowl, combine oil, sugar, salt, and spice.
3. Chop the tofu into about one inch cubes.
4. Place tofu into the bowl and gently combine them with the spice mix.
5. Put the tofu in the air fryer basket and ensure they aren't touching each other.
6. Cook for 15 minutes.
7. Then serve with soy sauce or Hoisin sauce.

Nutrition Values:

Calories: 140 | Carbohydrates: 7g | Fat: 6.9g | Saturated Fat: 0.7g | Sodium: 588mg | Fiber: 1.7g | Protein: 13.4g | Potassium: 57.6mg | Sugar: 1.4g

PHILLY CHEESESTEAK EMPANADAS

Preparation Time: 30 minutes | Cooking Time: 30 minutes | Servings: 2

Ingredients:

For filling:

- 1/2 cup RAGÚ Double Cheddar Sauce
- Canola oil (for sautéing)
- Salt and pepper
- 12 oz. rib-eye or sirloin steak (slice as thin as you can)
- 1 small yellow onion (chopped into thin half-rings)

For dough:

- 1 large egg
- 3 cups all-purpose flour and more as needed
- 1 cup water, warm
- 1/4 cup canola oil
- 1 teaspoon salt
- 1/2 teaspoon baking powder
- 1/2 teaspoon baking soda

For dipping:

- Red Duck Smoky Ketchup

Instructions:

Prepare the dough

1. In the bowl of the stand mixer, mix the baking soda, baking powder, salt and flour. Combine on low speed to distribute the ingredients.
2. As the mixer runs on low speed, add the water and oil. Increase the speed to medium and combine for three minutes.
3. Remove dough from the mixer and place on a well-floured work surface. Then knead for a few minutes while adding several tablespoonfuls of flour as needed till the dough is no longer sticky. Encase in plastic wrap and chill for half an hour.

Prepare the filling

1. Heat a large pan on medium-high heat. Pour in enough canola oil once hot to coat the pan's bottom. Place in the onion and then sauté for about 7 to 10 minutes. Add pepper and salt to taste. Transfer to a bowl.
2. Pour in additional oil if necessary. Place the sirloin or rib-eye onto the sauté pan. Shred thin pieces of meat while cooking with two spatulas. When close to finished (no longer

red), return the onions back to pan and combine. Add pepper and salt to taste. Place filling in a bowl.

Assembling the empanadas

1. Transfer dough from the fridge and allow to rest for 20 minutes while still wrapped. Divide the dough into twelve equal pieces. Then roll and pat each piece to form a circle about four inches in diameter.
2. Put two tablespoons of onion-meat filling in the middle of each dough circle. Top the meat with two teaspoons of RAGU Double Cheddar Sauce. Then fold one half of dough over filling till it nearly meets the opposite side. Fold up the exposed edge of bottom half of the dough over the top half. Then seal using a well-floured fork.

Cooking empanadas

1. Preheat the air fryer to 325 F for 20 minutes.
2. Beat the egg together with one tablespoonful water. Smear 4 of the empanadas with egg mixture and put in the air fryer basket. Cook for 8 minutes.
3. Using a spatula, transfer the empanadas onto a plate. Smear 4 more empanadas with egg mixture and cook for 8 minutes. Repeat this process with the remaining empanadas.
4. Lastly, serve with red duck smoky ketchup.

Nutrition Values:

Calories: 244 kcal | Carbohydrates: 25g | Cholesterol: 35mg | Saturated Fat: 2g | Sodium: 424mg | Fiber: 1g | Protein: 11g | Sugar: 1g

SEAFOOD

PERFECT AIR FRYER SALMON

Preparation Time: 5 minutes | Cooking Time: 7 minutes | Servings: 2

Ingredients:

- Lemon wedges
- Salt and coarse black pepper
- 2 teaspoons paprika
- 2 teaspoons olive oil or avocado oil
- 2 wild caught salmon fillets with comparable thickness, mine were 1-1/12-inches thick

Instructions:

1. Start by removing bones from the salmon if need be and leave the fish to rest for one hour on the counter. Brush each fillet with the olive oil and then season with pepper, salt and paprika.
2. Transfer the fillets into an air fryer basket. For 1 to ½ inch fillets, cook for 7 minutes at 390 F.
3. When time is done, open the basket and then check the fillets with fork to ensure they're done to your liking.

Nutrition Values:

Calories: 288 | Carbohydrates: 1.4g | Cholesterol: 78mg | Fat: 18.9g | Saturated Fat: 2.6g | Sodium: 80.6mg | Fiber: 0.8g | Protein: 28.3g | Potassium: 52.5mg | Sugar: 0.3g

Cooking Tips

The time for cooking salmon will vary based on the size of the fillets and the temperature of the fish. It's better to set the air fryer for lesser time to prevent overcooking.

AIR FRYER BANG BANG FRIED SHRIMP

Preparation Time: 10 minutes | Cooking Time: 20 minutes | Servings: 4

Ingredients:

- cooking spray
- salt and pepper as desired
- 1 pound raw shrimp, peeled and deveined
- McCormick's Grill Mates Montreal Chicken Seasoning as desired
- 1 egg white (3 tablespoon)
- 1 teaspoon paprika
- 3/4 cup panko bread crumbs
- 1/2 cup all-purpose flour

Bang bang sauce

- 1/4 cup sweet chili sauce
- 2 tablespoon Sriracha
- 1/3 cup plain non-fat Greek yogurt

Instructions:

1. Preheat the air fryer to 400 F.
2. Season your shrimp with seasonings.
3. Put the panko bread crumbs, egg whites and flour in three separate bowls.
4. Form a cooking stations. Dunk shrimp into the flour, then dip in egg whites and lastly in panko bread crumbs.
5. As you dip shrimp in egg whites, you don't have to submerge it. A light dab will do so that most of the flour remains on shrimp. The egg white should just adhere to panko crumbs.
6. Spritz shrimp with cooking spray. Avoid spraying directly on it since the panko may go flying. Be sure to keep distance.
7. Place shrimp in the basket of the air fryer and let to cook for four minutes. Open the basket and then turn it to the other side. Let to cook for about 4 minutes until crisp.

Bang bang sauce

1. In a small bowl, mix all the ingredients thoroughly.

Nutrition Values:

Calories: 242kcal | Carbohydrates: 32g| Fat: 1g | Protein: 37g

Cooking Tips

For best results, look for the biggest shrimp.

You can add plain non-fat Greek yogurt to your dipping sauce to boost protein intake.

Feel free to use standard breadcrumbs if it's hard to get panko breadcrumbs.

To have the shrimp extra crispy, cook for about 8 to 10 minutes.

"JEWISH STYLE" AIR FRYER SALMON CROQUETTES

Preparation Time: 55 minutes | Cooking Time: 10 minutes | Servings: 2

Ingredients:

- Freshly Ground Black Pepper - 1/4 teaspoon
- Kosher Salt (or to taste) - 1 teaspoon
- Lemon Juice - 2 teaspoons
- Italian Seasoning Blend - 2 teaspoons
- Chives chopped - 1 Tablespoon
- Matzo Meal - 2 Tablespoons
- Mayonnaise - 1/4 cup
- 2 large Eggs
- 1 small Yellow/Brown Onion (grated)
- 1 medium Carrots grated
- Bumble Bee Pink Salmon, bones/skin removed (2 cans) - 29.5 ounce

Instructions:

1. Combine Aioli together, transfer into an airtight container and then place in the fridge.
2. Remove bones and skin from the salmon and put in a medium bowl.
3. Peel the carrot and then grate. Transfer to the bowl with salmon.
4. Grate the onion squeeze the excess water out. Transfer to the bowl of salmon.
5. Add lemon, juice, chives, pepper, salt, Italian seasonings, matzo meal, mayonnaise and eggs. Combine everything together.
6. Divide into twelve portions and then roll into balls.
7. Flatten the balls out onto cookie sheet. Should be roughly three inches in diameter and ¾ inches thick.
8. Refrigerate the patties for half an hour.
9. In a single layer, put six patties in a greased air fryer and spritz well with oil.
10. Let to cook for six minutes at 400 F. Turn over.
11. Spritz once again with oil and cook for about four minutes until browned on each side.
12. Decorate with lemon zest and chives. Lastly, serve along with lemon dill aioli.

Nutrition Values:

Calories: 154 | Carbohydrates: 3g | Cholesterol: 95mg | Fat: 8g | Saturated Fat: 1g | Sodium: 506mg | Fiber: 1g | Protein: 18g | Potassium: 278mg | Sugar: 1g

Cooking Tips

You can replace Italian seasoning and matzo meal with Italian breadcrumbs.

AIR FRYER SALMON WITH DUKKAH CRUST

Preparation Time: 2 minutes | Cooking Time: 10 minutes | Servings: 2

Ingredients:

- 1 pinch salt
- 1 tablespoon dukkah
- 12 oz. salmon fillets

Instructions:

1. Preheat the air fryer to 390 degrees F.
2. Pat dry the salmon and get rid of the pin bones.
3. Add salt and drizzle one tablespoon dukkah over the fillets, skin side down.
4. Cut a square of baking paper that is large enough to fit the fillets. Put at the bottom of basket of the air fryer.
5. Put the salmon onto baking paper and then cook for about 10 to 12 minutes depending on the thickness of fillets.

Nutrition Values:

Calories: 251 | Carbohydrates: 1g | Cholesterol: 93mg | Fat: 11g | Saturated Fat: 1g | Sodium: 76mg | Protein: 33g | Potassium: 852mg

AIR FRYER SHRIMP EGG ROLLS

Preparation Time: 15 minutes | Cooking Time: 15 minutes | Servings: 5

Ingredients:

- 1 beaten egg
- 10 egg roll wrappers
- 10 large cooked shrimp (chopped into small pieces)
- 3 cups shredded cabbage or coleslaw mix
- 1/4 cup vegetable or chicken broth
- 1 tsp toasted sesame oil
- 1/2 tbsp. sugar
- 1 tsp fresh ground ginger
- 1 cup chopped carrots
- 2 tbsp. soy sauce
- 1/2 cup chopped green onion
- 3 minced garlic cloves

Instructions:

1. Heat oil in large skillet on top of medium heat. Add garlic and ginger and let to cook for 30 seconds.
2. Add green onion and carrots into the pan and sauté for two minutes.
3. In the meantime, whisk broth, sugar, and soy sauce together.
4. Stir in shrimp, coleslaw mix/cabbage and soy sauce mixture to the pan with veggies. Cook for five minutes.
5. Take out the pan from the heat source and let to cool for approx. 15 minutes. Then strain the liquid in a strainer.
6. While the coleslaw/vegetable mixture cools, preheat your air fryer to 390 degrees F.
7. Put egg roll wrappers onto a work surface. Add three tablespoons veggie/shrimp mixture on top of each.
8. Smear some egg on the edges of wrapper. Then roll up the wrappers and fold over the sides to contain the filling. Smear the egg onto the outside of each egg roll just before placing them in your air fryer. (The egg roll may get soft and can rip if you rub it on and leave to rest).
9. Spritz the basket of an air fryer with cooking spray. Gently place three to four egg rolls at a time into the basket of air fryer. Rub the tops of the egg rolls with egg.
10. Cook for about 8 to 9 minutes or until crunchy and brown on the outside.
11. Serve right away.

Nutrition Values:

Calories: 240 | Carbohydrates: 39g | Cholesterol: 80mg | Fat: 2g | Sodium: 913mg | Fiber: 2g | Protein: 12g | Sugar: 4g

AIR FRYER COCONUT SHRIMP

Preparation Time: 15 minutes | Cooking Time: 8 minutes | Servings: 2

Ingredients:

- 3 tbsp. all-purpose flour
- Dash Louisiana-style hot sauce
- Dash pepper
- 1/8 tsp salt
- 2 large egg whites
- 3 tbsp. panko bread crumbs
- 1/2 cup sweetened coconut, shredded
- 1/2 pound large shrimp, uncooked

SAUCE

- Dash crushed red pepper flakes
- 1/2 tsp cider vinegar
- 1/3 cup apricot preserves

Instructions:

1. Preheat your air fryer to 375 degrees F. Peel and devein the shrimp and leave the tails on.
2. Toss the coconut with the bread crumbs in a shallow bowl. Whisk hot sauce, pepper, salt and egg whites in another shallow bowl. Put the flour in the third shallow bowl.
3. Dunk the shrimp into the flour and coat lightly. Shake to remove excess. Dunk in the egg white mixture and then in the coconut mixture and pat to help the coating adhere.
4. In a single layer, transfer the shrimp onto greased tray in the basket of air fryer. Let to cook for four minutes. Flip the shrimp and continue to cook for 4 more minutes until the shrimp turns pink and coconut is lightly browned.
5. In the meantime, mix the sauce ingredients in small saucepan. Then cook while stirring over medium-low heat till the preserves have melted. You can serve the shrimp right away along with sauce.

Nutrition Values:

Calories: 423 | Carbohydrates: 59g | Cholesterol: 138mg | Fat: 10g | Saturated Fat: 8g | Sodium: 440mg | Fiber: 2g | Protein: 25g | Sugar: 34g

TOMATO BASIL SCALLOPS

Preparation Time: 5 minutes | Cooking Time: 10 minutes | Servings: 2

Ingredients:

- Cooking oil spray
- 3/4 cup (178.5 g) heavy whipping cream
- 8 jumbo sea scallops
- 1 tbsp. tomato paste
- 1 12 oz. Frozen Spinach (thawed and drained)
- 1 tsp minced garlic
- 1/2 tsp ground black pepper
- 1/2 tsp kosher salt
- 1 tbsp. chopped fresh basil
- More salt and pepper for seasoning scallops

Instructions:

1. Spritz a seven-inch heatproof pan and then add spinach to pan in an even layer.
2. Spritz each side of scallop with vegetable oil. Drizzle pepper and salt on top and transfer the scallops to pan, placing on top of spinach.
3. Combine the garlic, basil, pepper, salt, tomato paste and cream in a small bowl. Pour on top of scallops and spinach.
4. Cook for 10 minutes at 350 F until the sauce is hot and bubbling and scallops are cooked through. The internal temperature should be 135 degrees F.

Nutrition Values:

Calories: 359kcal | Carbohydrates: 6g | Fat: 33g | Protein: 9g | Sugar: 1g

ZESTY RANCH AIR FRYER FISH FILLETS

Preparation Time: 5 minutes | Cooking Time: 12 minutes | Servings: 4

Ingredients:

- 4 tilapia salmon or any other fish fillet
- 2 beaten eggs
- 2 1/2 tbsp. vegetable oil
- 1 30g packet dry ranch-style dressing mix
- 3/4 cup crushed cornflakes or bread crumbs or Panko
- Lemon wedges for garnish

Instructions:

1. Preheat the air fryer to 356 F.
2. Combine the ranch dressing mix and breadcrumbs/panko together. Pour in oil and keep stirring till the mixture is crumbly and loose.
3. Dunk the fillets in the egg and let the excess drip off.
4. Dredge the fish in the breadcrumb mixture and coat them evenly and thoroughly.
5. Transfer to the air fryer gently.
6. Let to cook for about 12 to 13 minutes depending on thickness of fish.
7. Take out and then serve. If you like, squeeze lemon wedges on top of the fish.

Nutrition Values:

Calories: 315kcal | Carbohydrates: 8g | Cholesterol: 166mg | Fat: 14g | Saturated Fat: 8g | Sodium: 220mg | Protein: 38g | Potassium: 565mg

AIR FRYER SOUTHERN FRIED CATFISH

Preparation Time: 15 minutes | Cooking Time: 13 minutes | Servings: 4

Ingredients:

- Yellow Mustard - 1/2 cup
- Lemon - 1
- Milk - 1 cup
- Catfish Fillets - 2 pounds

Cornmeal seasoning mix

- Cayenne pepper - 1/4 teaspoon
- Granulated onion powder - 1/4 teaspoon
- Garlic powder - 1/4 teaspoon
- Chili powder - 1/4 teaspoon
- Freshly ground black pepper - 1/4 teaspoon
- Cornmeal - 1/2 cup
- Kosher salt - 1/2 teaspoon
- Dried parsley flakes - 2 Tablespoons
- All-purpose flour - 1/4 cup

Instructions:

1. Put the catfish in a flat container and pour in milk.
2. Half the lemon and squeeze approximately two teaspoons juice into milk to make buttermilk.
3. Put the container in the fridge and leave the fillets to soak for 15 minutes.
4. Mix the cornmeal seasoning ingredients in a shallow bowl.
5. Take out the fillets from the buttermilk and then pat dry using paper towels.
6. Generously spread on each side of fillets.
7. Dunk each fillet in the cornmeal mixture and coat thoroughly to form a thick coating.
8. Put the fillets in a greased basket of the air fryer. Generously spray with oil.
9. Cook for ten minutes at 390/400 F. Turn over the fish and spritz with oil. Let cook for about 3 to 5 more minutes.

Nutrition Values:

Calories: 391 kcal | Carbohydrates: 29 g | Cholesterol: 138 mg | Fat: 11 g | Saturated Fat: 3 g | Sodium: 776 mg | Fiber: 4 g | Protein: 44 g | Potassium: 1063 mg | Sugar: 4 g

Cooking Tip

A combination of Dijon mustard and yellow mustard can also work well.

AIR FRYER KETO SALMON BOK CHOY RECIPE

Preparation Time: 20 minutes | Cooking Time: 12 minutes | Servings: 2

Ingredients:

- 2 five ounce (708.74 g) salmon fillets
- 1/2 tsp kosher salt
- 1 tbsp. vegetable oil
- 3 tbsp. rice vinegar
- 1/4 cup (58 ml) soy sauce
- 1/2 cup (124 ml) fresh orange juice
- 2 tsp finely grated orange zest
- 1 tbsp. minced ginger
- 2 minced garlic cloves

For veggies

- 1/2 tsp toasted sesame seeds
- Kosher salt
- 2 ounces (56.7 g) Dried stemmed Shiitake Mushrooms (discard stems)
- 2 heads baby bok choy (cut in half lengthwise)
- 1 tbsp. Dark sesame oil

Instructions:

1. Whisk vegetable oil, vinegar, salt, soy sauce, orange zest & juice, ginger and garlic together in a small bowl. Remove ½ of the marinade and set aside. Put the fish into a gallon-size resealable bag. Spread the remaining half marinade onto salmon. Seal the bag and massage to coat fish. Let to marinate for half an hour at lukewarm.
2. Transfer the fish to your air fryer and cook for 12 minutes at 400 F.
3. In the meantime, prepare the veggies. Rub mushroom caps and bok choy all over with sesame oil and sprinkle a little salt. After six minutes of cooking, add veggies around the fish in the basket of air fryer. Continue to cook for six minutes.
4. Sprinkle a little of the reserved marinade onto salmon and then drizzle sesame seeds over vegetables. Serve.

Nutrition Values:

Calories: 195 | Carbohydrates: 12 g | Fat: 14 g | Fiber: 1 g | Protein: 4 g | Sugar: 6 g

DINNER

CRISPY LOW-FAT FRIED CHICKEN

Preparation Time: 1 hour | Cooking Time: 30 minutes | Servings: 4

Ingredients:

- Buttermilk - 2 cups
- Seasoned flour like Kentucky kernel flour - 1 cup
- Oil for spraying
- 1 whole chicken, chopped up
- Hot sauce - 1 tablespoon

Instructions:

1. Combine hot sauce and buttermilk.
2. Put the chicken into a large bowl and then add buttermilk mixture. Place in the fridge for one hour.
3. Place the seasoned four in a plastic bag or large bowl. Then dredge the chicken in the flour.
4. Put the chicken in the air fryer basket. Then spritz with oil and let to cook for half an hour at 380 degrees F, turning chicken after 15 minutes and sprinkling the turned side with oil.

Nutrition Values:

Calories: 665kcal | Carbohydrates: 46g | Cholesterol: 156mg | Fat: 33g | Saturated Fat: 10g | Sodium: 3072mg | Protein: 44g | Potassium: 522mg | Sugar: 6g

20 MINUTE AIR FRYER CHICKEN BREAST

Preparation Time: 15 minutes | Cooking Time: 10 minutes | Servings: 4

Ingredients:

- Olive oil - 1 tablespoon
- Boneless skinless chicken breasts - 1 lb. (Roughly two large)

Breading

- Cayenne pepper - 1/16 teaspoon
- Onion powder - 1/8 teaspoon
- Garlic powder - 1/8 teaspoon
- Paprika - ½ teaspoon
- Black pepper - ¼ teaspoon
- Salt - ½ teaspoon
- Bread crumbs - ¼ cup

Instructions:

1. Heat an air fryer to 390 degrees F.
2. Cut the chicken breasts in half horizontally to have 2 thin breast halves from each.
3. Lightly smear each side with olive oil.
4. Combine the breading ingredients together. Then dredge chicken breasts into the breading several times till they're coated thoroughly.
5. Shake the chicken breasts to remove excess breading and transfer to the air fryer in a single layer. (Two breast halves at a time).
6. Let to cook for four minutes, turn and then cook for 2 minutes. Cooking time depends on the thickness and size of the chicken breasts. Therefore, you can use a digital thermometer to check whether the chicken meat has reached 165 degrees F or just slice one in half.

To make ahead: You can cook air fryer chicken breasts two to three days ahead and then store in your refrigerator. Return the chicken in your air fryer for two to three minutes until they're heated through and the breading is crispy once again.

Nutrition Values:

Calories: 188kcal | Carbohydrates: 5g | Cholesterol: 72mg | Fat: 6g | Saturated Fat: 1g | Sodium: 472mg | Protein: 25g | Potassium: 432mg

Cooking Tips

It's recommend to use regular breadcrumbs in place of panko since the seasonings usually mix in better.

AIR FRYER GARLIC PARMESAN CHICKEN TENDERS

Preparation Time: 5 minutes | Cooking Time: 12 minutes | Servings: 4

Ingredients:

- Non-fat cooking spray or canola
- 2 tbsp. water
- 1 egg
- 8 raw chicken tenders

For dredge coating

- 1/4 cup parmesan cheese
- 1/2 teaspoon onion powder
- 1 teaspoon garlic powder
- 1/4 teaspoon ground black pepper (more or less to taste)
- 1/2 teaspoon salt
- 1 cup panko breadcrumbs

Optional sauce

- 1 cup dipping sauce you love such as BBQ, Blue Cheese, Honey mustard, or Ranch Dressing.

Instructions:

1. Mix the dredge ingredients in a baking pan or shallow bowl that is large enough to fit pieces of chicken.
2. Add water and egg in another baking pan or shallow bowl and then whisk to combine.
3. Dunk the chicken in the egg wash and then dredge in the panko mixture.
4. Transfer the breaded chicken into your air fryer. Repeat this process with the remaining chicken.
5. Spritz a light coat of non-fat cooking spray or canola oil over the panko.
6. Set the air fryer to 400 F and cook for 12 minutes. Check the tenders when halfway through cook time and flip to brown the other side.

Nutrition Values:

Calories: 220 kcal | Carbohydrates: 13 g | Cholesterol: 109 mg | Fat: 6 g | Saturated Fat: 2 g | Sodium: 582 mg | Fiber: 1 g | Protein: 27 g | Potassium: 429 mg | Sugar: 1 g

LOW CARB AIR FRIED CHICKEN

Preparation Time: 20 minutes | Cooking Time: 30 minutes | Servings: 4

Ingredients:

- 1 cup low carb bread crumbs
- 2 beaten eggs
- 1/2 tablespoon of Seasoning
- 1 cup Carbalose
- 4 skinless chicken breast or any piece you love

Instructions:

1. Set up the dredging station with 3 shallow bowls. In the first bowl, blend or whisk the seasoning and flour together. Pour the eggs in the second bowl and put breadcrumbs in the third bowl.
2. In the meantime, lightly spray the air fryer basket with nonstick if desired and preheat your air fryer to 360 F.
3. Dredge each chicken piece, one at a time, in the flour and then shake to remove excess flour. Dip the chicken in egg, allowing the excess to drip off and then dredge in breadcrumbs. You can press or pat the crumbs into the meat.
4. Cook the meat for about 12 to 15 minutes. The meat should no longer be pink and the internal temperature should reach 329 degrees F. Repeat this with the remaining pieces of chicken.

Nutrition Values:

Calories: 175 kcal | Carbohydrates: 3 g | Cholesterol: 82 mg | Fat: 5 g | Saturated Fat: 1 g | Sodium: 1195 mg | Fiber: 2g | Protein: 18 g | Potassium: 54 mg | Sugar: 1 g

AIR-FRIED BURGERS

Preparation Time: 10 minutes | Cooking Time: 10 minutes | Servings: 4

Ingredients:

- 1 lb. (500 g) raw ground beef
- 1 tsp dried parsley
- 1/2 tsp ground black pepper
- 1 tbsp. Worcestershire sauce
- 1/2 tsp salt (or salt sub)
- 1/2 tsp onion powder
- 1 tsp Maggi seasoning sauce
- 1/2 tsp garlic powder
- Liquid smoke (few drops)

Instructions:

1. Spritz upper Actifry and set it aside. No need to spray if using an air fryer basket. In basket-type air fryers, the cooking temperature is usually 350 F.
2. Combine all the seasoning ingredients together in a small bowl.
3. Transfer the mix to beef in a large bowl.
4. Combine thoroughly but take care not to overwork since the beef may lead to tough burgers.
5. Divide the meat mixture into four and then shape into patties. Make an indent in the middle of each patty with your thumb to keep them from bunching up in the middle.
6. Place the tray into Actifry and spritz patty tops lightly.
7. Cook for ten for medium or to the desired doneness. You don't need to flip the patties.
8. You can serve hot on a bun along with your favorite side dishes.

Nutrition Values:

Calories: 148 kcal | Fat: 4.6 g | Protein: 24.2 g

MAKE LOADED POTATOES IN AN AIR FRYER

Preparation Time: 10 minutes | Cooking Time: 15 minutes | Servings: 2

Ingredients:

- Kosher salt – 1/8 tsp
- Reduced-fat sour cream – 2 tbsp.
- Reduced-fat Cheddar cheese, finely shredded – ½ ounce (approx. 2 tbsp.)
- Chopped fresh chives – 1 ½ tbsp.
- Center-cut bacon slices – 2
- Olive oil – 1 tsp
- Baby Yukon Gold potatoes – 11 ounces (approx. 8 two inches potatoes)

Instructions:

1. Start by tossing the potatoes with oil to coat. Transfer them to your air fryer and let to cook while stirring often for about 25 minutes at 350 degrees F until fork tender.
2. In the meantime, cook the bacon over medium heat in a medium skillet for about 7 minutes until crispy. Take out bacon from pan and crumble. Transfer the cooked potatoes onto a serving platter and lightly crush to split. Sprinkle with bacon drippings. Then top with crumbled bacon, sour cream, cheese, chives and salt.

Nutrition Values:

Calories: 199 | Carbohydrates: 26g | Fat: 7g | Saturated Fat: 3g | Sodium: 287mg | Fiber: 4g | Protein: 7g | Sugar: 3g

AIR FRYER BEEF EMPANADAS

Preparation Time: 10 minutes | Cooking Time: 16 minutes | Servings: 8

Ingredients:

- 1 tsp water
- 1 egg white (whisked)
- 1 cup picadillo
- 8 Goya empanada discs, in frozen section (thawed)

Instructions:

1. Preheat your air fryer for 8 minutes to 325 F. Generously coat air fryer basket with cooking spray.
2. Put two tablespoons picadillo in the middle of each disc. Then fold in half and seal the edges with a fork. Repeat this with remaining dough.
3. Whisk egg whites and water together and then rub the tops of empanadas.
4. Cook for 8 minutes in air fryer, about 2 or 3 at time or until they're golden. Remove from the heat and repeat this with remaining empanadas.

Nutrition Values:

Calories: 183 | Carbohydrates: 22g | Cholesterol: 16mg | Fat: 5g | Saturated Fat: 1g | Sodium: 196mg Fiber: 1g | Protein: 11g | Sugar: 2.5g

CHICKEN PARMESAN IN THE AIR FRYER

Preparation Time: 20 minutes | Cooking Time: 10 minutes | Servings: 4

Ingredients:

- 1 package spaghetti
- 1 jar Marinara sauce
- Olive oil cooking spray
- Salt and pepper
- 3/4 cup marinara sauce
- 3 beaten eggs
- 1/2 cup shredded mozzarella cheese
- 1/2 cup grated parmesan cheese
- 1 cup panko bread crumbs
- 4 chicken breasts, skinless, thinly sliced

Instructions:

1. Preheat your air fryer to 460 degrees F.
2. Spritz air fryer basket with cooking spray if called for by your machine.
3. Put chicken breasts onto a hard surface.
4. In a large bowl mix the seasonings, parmesan, and panko breadcrumbs. Stir to combine.
5. Put eggs in a bowl and then beat until frothy.
6. Dunk chicken in egg and then dip in crumbs mixture.
7. Set aside.
8. Transfer the chicken to air fryer.
9. Spritz olive oil cooking spray on top of chicken.
10. Let cook for seven minutes.
11. Put chicken in a baking sheet.
12. Set the oven to broil on high.
13. Add the shredded mozzarella and marinara sauce on top of each breasts.
14. Let to cook for three minutes until the cheese melts.
15. Cook spaghetti according to the directions on the package.
16. When cooked, toss noodles into the leftover marinara.
17. Put the cooked chicken atop noodles.

Nutrition Values:

Calories: 600 | Carbohydrates: 67g | Cholesterol: 217mg | Fat: 14g | Saturated Fat: 6g | Sodium: 1850mg | Protein: 48g | Potassium: 1454mg | Sugar: 13g

AIR FRYER CHICKEN NUGGETS

Preparation Time: 15 minutes | Cooking Time: 8 minutes | Servings: 4

Ingredients:

- 2 tbsp. parmesan cheese, grated
- 2 tbsp. panko
- 6 tbsp. whole wheat Italian seasoned breadcrumbs
- 2 tsp olive oil
- 1/2 tsp black pepper and kosher salt
- 16 oz. two large chicken breasts (skinless and boneless) sliced into even one-inch bite sized pieces
- Olive oil spray

Instructions:

1. Preheat your air fryer for 8 minutes to 400 degrees F.
2. In one bowl, add olive oil and in another bowl place the parmesan cheese, panko and breadcrumbs.
3. Season the chicken with pepper and salt. Transfer to the bowl of olive oil and combine thoroughly to evenly coat the meat with oil.
4. Place a few chunks of the chicken in the crumb mixture to coat. Then transfer to the basket.
5. Spray the top lightly using olive oil spray and cook for 8 minutes, flipping halfway till golden.

Nutrition Values:

Calories: 188 | Carbohydrates: 8g | Cholesterol: 57mg | Fat: 4.5g | Saturated Fat: 1g | Sodium: 427mg | Protein: 25g | Sugar: 0.5g

AIR FRYER STUFFED PEPPERS

Preparation Time: 15 minutes | Cooking Time: 15 minutes | Servings: 1

Ingredients:

- 1/4 cup mozzarella cheese, shredded
- 1 cup marinara sauce
- 6 green bell peppers
- 1 cup cooked rice
- 1 lb. lean ground beef
- 1/2 teaspoon Garlic Salt
- 1/2 teaspoon ground sage
- 1 tablespoon olive oil
- 1/4 cup fresh parsley
- 1/4 cup green diced onion

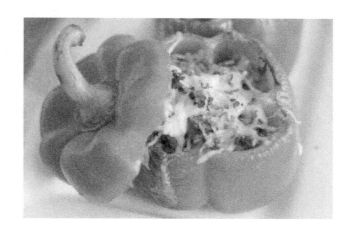

Instructions:

1. Cook the ground beef in a medium sized skillet until it is well done.
2. Drain the meat and place back in the pan.
3. Pour in the sage, salt, parsley, green onion, and olive oil. Combine well.
4. Place in marinara and cooked rice and combine well.
5. Chop off the top of each pepper and remove the seeds.
6. Stuff the mixture into each pepper and then transfer to the air fryer basket.
7. Air fry at 355 F for 10 minutes. Gently open and add cheese.
8. Continue to cook for 5 more minutes or until the cheese has melted and the peppers become slightly soft.
9. Lastly, serve

Nutrition Values:

Calories: 296 | Carbohydrates: 19g | Cholesterol: 70mg | Fat: 13g | Saturated Fat: 4g | Sodium: 419mg | Fiber: 2g | Protein: 25g | Sugar: 6g

SIDE DISH

CHEESY POTATO WEDGES

Preparation Time: 15 minutes | Cooking Time: 20 minutes | Servings: 4

Ingredients:

Potatoes

- Garlic powder - 1/2 teaspoon
- Ground black pepper - 1 teaspoon
- Salt - 1 teaspoon
- Olive oil - 1 teaspoon
- Fingerling potatoes - 1 pound

Cheese sauce

- Water - 2 tablespoons to ¼ cup
- Lemon juice - 1 teaspoon
- Nutritional yeast - 2 tablespoons
- Paprika - ½ teaspoon
- Turmeric - ½ teaspoon
- Raw cashews - ½ cup

Instructions:

1. For potatoes: Start by preheating your air fryer to 400 degrees F for three minutes. Wash potatoes, then chop in half lengthwise and place them in a large bowl. Add garlic power, pepper, salt and oil to potatoes. Toss to coat the potatoes. Put potatoes in your air fryer and let to cook for sixteen minutes, shaking when halfway through cooking time.
2. For Cheese sauce: In a high-speed blender, mix lemon juice, nutritional yeast, paprika, turmeric, and cashews. Then blend on low gradually increasing the speed and adding water as needed. Take care to avoid adding too much water since you want a thick cheesy consistency.
3. Place cooked potatoes in a piece of parchment paper or in the air fryer-safe pan. Sprinkle cheese sauce on top of potato wedges. Put pan in an air fryer and then cook at 400 degrees F for two minutes.

Nutrition Values:

Calories: 182kcal | Carbohydrates: 21g | Fat: 8g | Saturated Fat: 1g | Sodium: 595mg | Fiber: 4g | Protein: 7g | Potassium: 649mg | Sugar: 1g

Cooking Tips

You can omit olive oil.

It's recommended to use Phillips Air Fryer.

AIR FRYER POTATO CHIPS

Preparation Time: 30 minutes | Cooking Time: 15 minutes | Servings: 6

Ingredients:

- Minced fresh parsley, if desired
- 1/2 tsp sea salt
- Olive oil-flavored cooking spray
- 2 large potatoes

Instructions:

1. Preheat your air fryer to 360 degrees F. Chop the potatoes into very thin slices with a vegetable peeler or mandolin. Place in a large bowl and pour in enough ice water to cover the slices. Let to soak for 15 minutes and then drain. Pour in ice water once again and leave to soak for 15 minutes.
2. Drain your potatoes and transfer onto towels to pat dry. Spray the slices with cooking spray and then drizzle with salt. Working in batches, arrange the slices in a single layer on the tray in the greased basket of air-fryer. Let to cook for about 15 to 17 minutes until golden brown and crisp, stirring and flipping after every 5 to 7 minutes. Drizzle with parsley if desired

Nutrition Values:

Calories: 148 | Carbohydrates: 32g | Cholesterol: 0mg | Fat: 1g | Sodium: 252mg | Fiber: 4g | Protein: 4g | Sugar: 2g

CRISPY AIR FRYER FRENCH FRIES

Preparation Time: 15 minutes | Cooking Time: 15 minutes | Servings: 4

Ingredients:

- Paprika - 1/2 teaspoon
- Garlic powder - 1/4 teaspoon
- Fine sea salt - 1/2 teaspoon
- Extra-virgin olive oil - 1 tablespoon
- Scrubbed Russet or Yukon Gold potatoes - 1 pound

Instructions:

1. Preheat your air fryer to 375 degrees F. Slice potatoes into French fry shapes, roughly ¼ inch thick. Transfer the potato slices into a bowl with warm water and leave them to sit for ten minutes.
2. Drain your potatoes, then pat dry and put them into a large bowl. Sprinkle olive oil atop potatoes. Season with the paprika, garlic powder and salt. Combine well to coat your potatoes.
3. Spread the slices of potatoes in the basket of your air fryer in a single layer if you can. You can cook in two batches. They will become crispier the more separated.
4. Let cook for 15 minutes at 375 degrees F. After 10 minutes of cooking, toss the fries to crisp them evenly. Then serve warm along with dipping sauce you like.

You can place leftover fries in an airtight container and then store in the refrigerator for four days maximum. They may get soggy after storage. You should reheat in your air fryer prior to serving to crisp them again.

Nutrition Values:

Calories: 80 | Carbohydrates: 10g | Fat: 3g | Sodium: 8mg | Fiber: 2g | Protein: 2g | Potassium: 351mg

AIR FRYER BAKED POTATO RECIPE

Preparation Time: 3 minutes | Cooking Time: 35 minutes | Servings: 1

Ingredients:

For baked potato

- 1/8 teaspoon coarse salt
- 1/4 teaspoon onion powder
- 1 teaspoon organic canola oil
- 1 medium Russet potato

Baked potato topping

- Chopped chives, if desired for garnish
- Pepper as desired
- Salt as desired
- Dollop vegan butter

Instructions:

1. Make holes in your Russet potato with a fork or knife. Brush it with coarse salt, onion powder and oil. Transfer to your air fryer.
2. Cook for about 35 to 40 minutes at 390 F, flipping once when halfway done. Time will depend on the size of the potato. You can decrease the temperature to 370 F if potato becomes too dark on the outside. Potato is done when fork easily pokes inside.
3. Slice through potato, then fluff the interior using fork and add your favorite toppings.

Nutrition Values:

Calories: 205 | Carbohydrates: 38g | Fat: 4g | Sodium: 301mg | Fiber: 2g | Protein: 4g | Potassium: 888mg | Sugar: 1g

Cooking Tips

This recipe uses one potato but you can use four since many air fryers can accommodate up to four Russet potatoes. Make sure not to overfill since air flow is necessary to achieve best results.

AIR FRYER ROAST VEGETABLES

Preparation Time: 5 minutes | Cooking Time: 10 minutes | Servings: 4

Ingredients:

- ½ teaspoon spice or herb mix, if desired
- ¼ small pumpkin
- 1 large carrot
- 1 large potato
- 1 large sweet potato

Instructions:

1. Peel the veggies or wash them if preferred. Chop into chunks of not thicker than one inch. Pat dry the veggies.
2. Transfer the veggies to the basket of your air fryer and spritz with olive oil. If you like, add spice. Then shake and spritz with oil once again.
3. Let to cook for five minutes in your air fryer at 360 degrees F. Take out the basket and shake.
4. Place back into air fryer and let to cook for about 5 to 10 more minutes till golden.

Nutrition Values:

Calories: 156 | Carbohydrates: 35g | Sodium: 69mg Fiber: 5g | Protein: 4g | Potassium: 1014mg | Sugar: 6g

AIR FRYER CORN

Preparation Time: 2 minutes | Cooking Time: 15 minutes | Servings: 4

Ingredients:

- Olive oil spray
- 2 corn cobs

Instructions:

1. Preheat your air fryer to 360 degrees F.
2. Remove husk from your corn and then slice each into two pieces.
3. Transfer the cobs to the air fryer and then spritz with olive oil.
4. Let to cook for 12 to 15 minutes until they start to become golden brown.
5. Remove from the machine and serve.

Nutrition values:

Calories: 38.7 | Carbohydrates: 8.4g | Fat: 0.6g | Saturated Fat: 0.1g | Sodium: 6.8mg | Fiber: 0.9g | Protein: 1.5g | Potassium: 121.5mg | Sugar: 2.8g

AIR FRYER CARROTS

Preparation Time: 5 minutes | Cooking Time: 10 minutes | Servings: 4

Ingredients:

- 1 teaspoon thyme (fresh or dried)
- 1 tablespoon olive oil
- 1 tablespoon butter
- 4 medium carrots

Instructions:

1. Preheat the air fryer to 360 degrees F.
2. Chop the carrots lengthwise into quarters.
3. In a large microwave safe bowl, put butter and then heat in microwave for about 10 to 15 seconds until it is melted.
4. Add thyme and olive oil to melted butter and stir to combine.
5. Place the pieces of carrots into the butter/oil mixture and then toss to coat well.
6. Transfer the coated carrots to the air fryer and let to cook for about 10 to 15 minutes.
7. Carrots are done after turning golden brown and when tender.

Nutrition Values:

Calories: 81.5 | Carbohydrates: 6g | Cholesterol: 7.5mg | Fat: 6.5g | Saturated Fat: 2.3g | Sodium: 67.2mg | Protein: 0.6g | Potassium: 195.2mg | Sugar: 2.9g

AIR FRYER CAULIFLOWER

Preparation Time: 1 hour | Cooking Time: 30 minutes | Servings: 4

Ingredients:

- Pesto - 2 tablespoon
- Flaked toasted almonds - ¼ cup
- Salt - ½ tsp
- Paprika - 1 tsp
- Turmeric - 1 tsp
- Olive oil - ¼ cup
- Cauliflower - 1 head

Instructions:

1. Chop the cauliflower into florets.
2. In a large bowl, put paprika, salt, turmeric and olive oil. Combine.
3. Place the cauliflower into the bowl and combine gently to ensure each floret in coated well with spice/oil mixture.
4. Transfer the cauliflower to the basket of air fryer and cook for 15 minutes at 360 degrees F.
5. Take out from the air fryer, top with pesto sprinkle and flaked almonds and serve.

Nutrition Values:

Calories: 226.3 | Carbohydrates: 9.8g | Cholesterol: 0.6mg | Fat: 20.1g | Saturated Fat: 2.7g | Sodium: 404.8mg | Fiber: 4.1g | Protein: 4.7g | Potassium: 501.4mg | Sugar: 3.3g

AIR FRYER PUMPKIN

Preparation Time: 2 minutes | Cooking Time: 10 minutes | Servings: 4

Ingredients:

- ½ tsp nutmeg or any other spice, if desired
- Olive oil spray
- 2 lb. pumpkin (you can use precut ones from stores)

Instructions:

1. Preheat the air fryer to 360 degrees F.
2. Chop the pumpkin into chunks or wedges of about half inch thick.
3. Put the pieces of pumpkin into the basket of your air fryer. Spread the pieces without touching each other in the basket if possible. Otherwise, make sure you shake the basket when halfway through cook time.
4. Spritz olive oil onto the pumpkin.
5. Drizzle nutmeg or other spices atop pumpkin if desired.
6. Transfer the basket into the air fryer and roast for 10 minutes. Pumpkin is done when golden and tender.

Nutrition Values:

Calories: 32 kcal | Carbohydrates: 7g | Fat: 1g | Saturated Fat: 1g | Sodium: 1mg | Fiber: 1g | Protein: 1g | Potassium: 386mg | Sugar: 3g

AIR FRYER ROASTED TOMATOES

Preparation Time: 2 minutes | Cooking Time: 10 minutes | Servings: 2

Ingredients:

- 1 spray olive oil
- 8 cherry tomatoes or 4 small tomatoes

Instructions:

1. Slice your tomatoes in half and put into a small baking dish. You can also air fry whole cherry tomatoes.
2. Spritz olive oil onto the tomatoes.
3. Place tomatoes in the air fryer and let to for ten minutes at 350 degrees F until they are tender.

Nutrition Values:

Calories: 37 | Carbohydrates: 7g | Fat: 1g | Saturated Fat: 1g | Sodium: 9mg | Protein: 2g | Potassium: 431mg | Sugar: 5g

SNACKS

SIMPLE BLACK BEAN BURGER

Preparation Time: 10 minutes | Cooking Time: 25 minutes | Servings: 6

Ingredients:

- 1/2 cup corn kernels (fresh or frozen and thawed) optional
- 1/2 tsp of garlic powder
- 1/4-1/2 tsp of chipotle chile powder (or to taste)
- 1 1/4 tsp of mild chili powder
- 1 tbsp. of soy sauce (or 1/2 teaspoon salt, if desired)
- 3/4 cup salsa
- 16 ounces black beans (1 can, drained well)
- 1 1/3 cups rolled oats, old fashioned ones, (make burgers gluten-free by using certified gluten-free oats)

Instructions:

1. Put your oats in the food processor that is attached with an S-blade and then pulse for about five or six times till partially chopped (some will be whole while others powder). Place in all of the ingredients apart from corn and process till most of the beans become blended.
2. Transfer the bean mixture to a bowl and mix in corn. Cover the bowl and place in a fridge for approximately 15 minutes.
3. Preheat the oven to 375 degrees F. Line parchment paper onto a baking sheet. Shape the bean mixture into 6 patties with a scant half cup for each. Then bake for about 20 to 30 minutes, taking care not to overcook and dry patties out. Once they start to become crispy and hold together, they are done.

Instructions for air fryer

1. Preheat your air fryer to about 375 degrees F. Arrange burgers in the basket of air fryer, in a single layer and cook for around 15 minutes until they are crispy slightly on the outside. In most cases, they will stick and hence, consider to use perforated parchment paper below them.

Nutrition Values:

Calories: 158kcal | Carbohydrates: 30g | Fat: 1.3g | Sodium: 690mg | Fiber: 9g | Protein: 8g | Potassium: 351mg | Sugar: 2.7g

CRISPY AIR FRYER SWEET POTATO TOTS

Preparation Time: 10 minutes | Cooking Time: 12 minutes | Servings: 25

Ingredients:

- Spray oil
- Regular breadcrumbs or panko breadcrumbs - 1/2 cup
- Coriander - 1/2 teaspoon
- Cumin - 1/2 teaspoon
- Salt - 1/2 teaspoon
- Sweet potato puree - 2 cups

Instructions:

1. Preheat the air fryer to 390 degrees F.
2. Combine all the ingredients together in a large bowl.
3. Shape into one tablespoon tots, use a cookie scoop, and then place on one to two plates.
4. Spritz with oil and be sure to coat the bottom of the tots with oil.
5. Gently arrange the tots in the basket of air fryer and leave space between them. You will need to cook in two or three batches.
6. Let to cook for 6 to 7 minutes and then flip them over gently. In case tots are very soft and mushy when flipping them, let them cook for a few minutes.
7. Continue to cook for about 5 to 7 minutes till each slide is crispy and not burned.
8. Serve right away with chipotle mayo, ketchup or guacamole.

To make ahead and freeze

1. Make the tots and spread in a baking sheet. Place in a freezer for a few hours till the tots are frozen. Place in a large freezer bag and then remove as much air as you can.
2. Cooking from frozen: preheat your air fryer to 390 degrees F.
3. Spritz frozen tots with oil and be sure to coat all sides.
4. Gently spread the tots in the basket of air fryer and leave space between them. Let to cook for nine to ten minutes and then gently flip them over. If tots are very soft and mushy as you flip them, let to sit for a few more minutes.
5. Cook for around five more minutes till each side is crispy and not burned.
6. Serve right away with chipotle mayo, ketchup or guacamole.

To bake in oven (for thawed or frozen tots)

1. Spray oil into a baking pan and then arrange the tots. Spritz the tots with oil.
2. Bake tots at 425 degrees F for 20 minutes.
3. Broil for about three to five minutes until crispy. Do not use parchment paper below the broiler.
4. Let to cool a bit before you remove from the baking sheet since they can stick when hot.

Nutrition Values:

Calories: 26 | Carbohydrates: 6g | Sodium: 32mg | Fiber: 2g | Protein: 1g | Sugar: 2g

AIR FRYER SIMPLE GRILLED AMERICAN CHEESE SANDWICH

Preparation Time: 2 minutes | Cooking Time: 8 minutes | Servings: 1

Ingredients:

- Mayonnaise or butter – 2 tsp
- Cheddar cheese – 2 to 3 slices
- Sandwich – 2 slices

Instructions:

Air fryer instructions

1. Put the cheese in between the bread slices and butter on the outside of each slice.
2. Transfer the slices into the air fryer and let cook for 8 minutes at 370 F. Turn when halfway through.

Crisplid instructions

1. Put cheese in between the bread slices and rub butter on the outside of each slice.
2. Put a tall trivet in the pressure cooker and put a crisplid basket at the top.
3. Transfer sandwich to the basket of crisplid and put crisplid at the top of the pressure cooker.
4. Let cook for 8 minutes at 400 degrees F, turning over after five minutes.

Nutrition Values:

Calories: 429 | Carbohydrates: 25g | Cholesterol: 80mg | Fat: 28g | Saturated Fat: 17g | Sodium: 664mg | Fiber: 1g | Protein: 18g | Potassium: 112mg

Cooking Tip

You can use your favorite cheese and stuff with tomatoes if you like.

AVOCADO FRIES IN AN AIR FRYER

Preparation Time: 15minutes | Cooking Time: 8 minutes | Servings: 4

Ingredients:

- Sriracha chili sauce - 1 tablespoon
- Apple cider vinegar - 1 tablespoon
- Canola mayonnaise - 2 tablespoons
- No-salt-added ketchup - 1/4 cup
- Cooking spray
- Kosher salt - 1/4 teaspoon
- 2 avocados, slice into 8 wedges each
- Water - 1 tablespoon
- 2 eggs, large
- Black pepper - 1 1/2 teaspoons
- All-purpose flour - 1/2 cup (about 2 1/8 oz.)
- Panko (Japanese-style breadcrumbs) - 1/2 cup

Instructions:

1. In a shallow dish, mix pepper and flour together. In another shallow dish, lightly beat the eggs and water. Put panko in the third dish. Dip the avocado wedges in the flour and shake off the excess. Then dunk in egg mixture and let the excess drip off. Dredge in the panko and press to adhere. Coat the wedges properly with cooking spray.
2. Transfer the wedges into the basket of air fryer and cook for about 7 to 8 minutes at 400 degrees F until golden. Flip the wedges over when halfway through cooking. Transfer from the air fryer and drizzle salt.
3. As the avocado cooks, whisk Sriracha, vinegar, mayonnaise, and ketchup together in a small bowl. To serve put four avocado fries onto each plate along with two tablespoons of sauce.

Nutrition Values:

Calories: 262 | Carbohydrates: 23g | Fat: 18g | Saturated Fat: 3g | Sodium: 306mg | Fiber: 7g | Protein: 5g | Sugar: 1g

AIR-FRYER REUBEN CALZONES

Preparation Time: 1 hour | Cooking Time: 30 minutes | Servings: 4

Ingredients:

- Thousand Island salad dressing
- Sliced cooked corned beef – ½ pound
- Sauerkraut (rinsed and well drained) – 1 cup
- Swiss cheese – 4 slices
- Refrigerated pizza crust – 13.8 ounces (1 tube)

Instructions:

1. Preheat the air fryer to 400 degrees. Unroll the pizza dough on a lightly floured surface and then pat into a twelve inch square. Slice into four squares. Spread diagonally one slice of cheese and a fourth of sauerkraut and the corned beef over half of every square to within half inch of edges. Then fold one corner over the filling to the other corner to make a triangle. Seal by pressing the edges with fork. Put two calzones on a greased tray in a single layer in the air fryer basket.
2. Let cook for about 8 to 12 minutes until golden brown. Turn when halfway through cooking. Then serve along with salad dressing.

Nutrition Values:

Calories: 430 | Carbohydrates: 49g | Cholesterol: 66mg | Fat: 17g | Saturated Fat: 6g | Sodium: 1471mg | Protein: 21g | Fiber: 2g | Sugar: 7g

DOUBLE-GLAZED AIR-FRIED CINNAMON BISCUIT BITES

Preparation Time: 15 minutes | Cooking Time: 10 minutes | Servings: 4

Ingredients:

- Water - 3 tablespoons
- Powdered sugar - 2 cups (approx. 8 oz.)
- Whole milk Cooking spray - 1/3 cup
- Cold salted butter, chopped into small pieces - 4 tablespoons
- Kosher salt - 1/4 teaspoon
- Ground cinnamon - 1/4 teaspoon
- Baking powder - 1 teaspoon
- Granulated sugar - 2 tablespoons
- Whole-wheat flour - 2/3 cup (approx. 2 2/3 oz.)
- All-purpose flour - 2/3 cup (approx. 2 7/8 oz.)

Instructions:

1. In a medium bowl, whisk together the cinnamon, salt, baking powder, granulated sugar and flours. Place in butter, chop into the mixture with a pastry cutter or two knives until the butter is well mixed with the flour and the mixture resembles coarse cornmeal. Pour in milk and mix together until the dough forms a ball. Put the dough on a floured surface and then knead for about 30 seconds until it is smooth and forms a cohesive ball. Divide the dough into 16 equal pieces. Then carefully roll each piece into a smooth ball.
2. Coat the basket of air fryer well with cooking spray. Put eight balls in the basket and leave space between each. Spritz the donut balls with cooking spray. Let cook for about 10 to 12 minutes at 350 degrees F until puffed and browned. Carefully transfer the donut from the basket to a wire rack over foil. Allow to cool for five minutes. Repeat this with the other donut balls.
3. In a medium bowl, whisk together water and powdered sugar until smooth. Carefully spoon half of glaze atop the donut balls. Allow to cool for five minutes and then glaze again. Let the excess drip off.

Nutrition Values:

Calories: 325 | Carbohydrates: 60g | Fat: 7g | Saturated Fat: 4g | Sodium: 67mg | Fiber: 5g | Protein: 8g | Sugar: 18g

AIR FRYER BUFFALO CAULIFLOWER BITES WITH GARLIC BLUE CHEESE DIP

Preparation Time: 40 minutes | Cooking Time: 16 minutes | Servings: 4-6

Ingredients:

Garlic blue cheese dip

- 1-2 tbsp. whole milk, buttermilk or heavy cream
- Freshly ground black pepper kosher salt and, as desired
- 1/4 cup crumbled blue cheese, freshly
- 1 grated clove of fresh garlic,
- 1 tbsp. minced fresh parsley
- 1 tbsp. snipped fresh chives, and more for garnish
- 1/4 cup sour cream
- 1/2 cup mayonnaise

Air fryer cauliflower bites

- Homemade Buffalo Sauce
- Freshly ground black pepper
- Kosher salt
- Olive oil spray
- 1 large head cauliflower, cut into bite-size florets

Instructions:

1. Combine together the garlic, parsley, chives, sour cream, and mayo in a medium bowl. Mix well. Place in blue cheese and season to taste with black pepper and salt. Then thin out with one to two tablespoons of either heavy cream, whole milk or buttermilk until the dip reaches the desired consistency. Cover tightly and then place in a fridge for at least 30 minutes to 1 hour in advance.
2. Spritz the air fryer basket with olive oil spray and then preheat to 390 to 400 degrees F, depending on your machine.
3. Spritz cauliflower florets with few sprays of olive oil and then season with freshly ground black pepper and kosher salt.
4. Working in two batches, place half of florets in the basket of air fryer. Cook for four minutes, shake and continue to cook for four minutes. Place the florets in a clean bowl before you repeat with the next batch.
5. When second batch is done, shake before returning first batch into basket of air fryer with second batch. Cook for about 2 to 4 minutes.
6. Place golden cauliflower into a large bowl.
7. Sprinkle some buffalo sauce atop the cauliflower and toss to coat. Serve together with garlic blue cheese dip.

Nutrition Values:

Calories: 273 | Carbohydrates: 8g | Cholesterol: 36mg | Fat: 24g | Saturated Fat: 7g | Sodium: 370mg | Fiber: 3g | Protein: 8g | Sugar: 4g

EASY SPRING ROLLS (AIR FRIED)

Preparation Time: 35 minutes | Cooking Time: 14 minutes | Servings: 20

Ingredients:

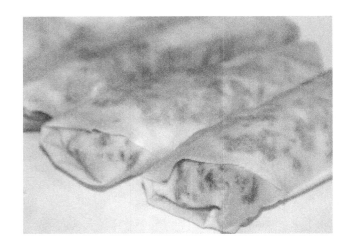

- 1 tbsp. vegetable oil or as desired
- 1 (16 ounce) package egg roll wrappers
- 1 tsp soy sauce
- 3 crushed cloves garlic
- 1 small diced onion
- 1 cup frozen mixed veggies
- 7 ounces ground beef
- 1 tbsp. sesame oil
- 2 ounces dried rice noodles

Instructions:

1. Start by soaking the rice noodles in a bowl with hot for about 5 minutes until soft. Chop the noodles into shorter strands.
2. In a wok, heat sesame oil over medium-high heat. Add garlic, onion, mixed veggies and ground beef. Cook for about six minutes until the beef is nearly browned throughout. Transfer from heat. Mix in noodles and allow to sit till the juices are absorbed. Pour soy sauce onto the filling.
3. Preheat the air fryer to 350 F.
4. Spread out one egg roll wrapper on a flat work surface. Put a diagonal strip of the filling across the wrapper. Then fold top corner over filling. Fold in the 2 side corners. Rub the middle with cold water and then roll over the spring roll to seal. Repeat this with remaining filling and wrappers.
5. Rub vegetable oil onto the tops of spring rolls. Place a batch of spring rolls in the air fryer basket and then cook for about 8 minutes until lightly browned and crisped. Repeat this till all are cooked.

Nutrition Values:

Calories: 112kcal | Carbohydrates: 16.4g | Cholesterol: 8mg | Fat: 3.2g | Sodium: 155mg | Protein: 4.1g

Cooking Tips

Feel free to use your favorite Asian noodles.

You can use frozen mixed veggies instead of fresh ones.

You can air fry the spring rolls without rubbing with oil. The oil just helps to give them a more familiar traditional taste.

You can also bake the spring rolls. First preheat your oven to 350 F. Arrange the rolls in a baking sheet and then bake for six minutes. Flip and bake for six minutes.

AIR FRYER PIZZA LOGS (HOMEMADE)

Preparation Time: 5 minutes | Cooking Time: 5 minutes | Servings: 10

Ingredients:

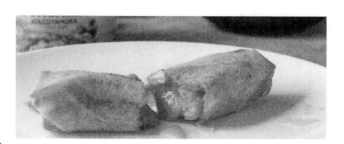

- 1 cup shredded cheese (mozzarella, pizza cheese)
- 1 cup (8 oz. jar)pizza sauce
- Olive oil spray
- 10 egg roll wrappers
- Other fillings, finely chopped (you can use ham, mushrooms, pepperoni)

Instructions:

1. Put the egg roll wrapper on a counter with a corner point at you.
2. Add one tablespoon cheese and one tablespoon sauce in the middle of egg roll wrapper.
3. If desired, add one tablespoon of any other toppings.
4. Roll front corner of egg roll wrapper over filling. Fold in the 2 sides of egg roll wrapper. Moisten slightly the top corner of the egg roll and continue to roll up to seal the pizza log.
5. Repeat this process to make pizza logs you want.
6. Put the pizza logs in the basket of air fryer and ensure they aren't touching each other. Spritz with olive oil spray.
7. Cook for five minutes at 360 degrees F until golden brown.

Nutrition Values:

Calories: 77.31 | Carbohydrates: 9.09g | Cholesterol: 10.02mg | Fat: 2.74g | Saturated Fat: 1.51g | Sodium: 272.96mg | Fiber: 0.6g | Protein: 4.08g | Potassium: 100.27mg | Sugar: 1.16g

AIR FRYER TOAST PIZZA

Preparation Time: 2 minutes | Cooking Time: 5 minutes | Servings: 1

Ingredients:

- 1 oz. shredded cheese
- 1 teaspoon tomato puree
- 1 slice bread (use thick-sliced)

Instructions:

1. Evenly pour one tablespoon tomato puree on the bread. Add cheese on top.
2. Transfer into the basket of air fryer and cook for five minutes at 390 degrees F until cheese starts to brown.

Nutrition Values:

Calories: 162 | Carbohydrates: 14g | Cholesterol: 22mg | Fat: 7g | Saturated Fat: 3g | Sodium: 324mg | Fiber: 1g | Protein: 9g | Potassium: 50mg | Sugar: 2g

DESSERTS

BLUEBERRY APPLE CRUMBLE

Preparation Time: 15 minutes | Cooking Time: 15 minutes | Servings: 2

Ingredients:

- 2 tbsp. nondairy butter
- 1/2 tsp ground cinnamon
- 2 tbsp. sugar
- 1/4 cup and 1 tbsp. brown rice flour
- 1/2 cup blueberries strawberries or peaches (frozen)
- 1 medium apple, finely diced

Instructions:

1. Preheat your air fryer to 350 degrees F for five minutes. Mix the frozen blueberries and apple in the air fryer-safe ramekin or baking pan.
2. Combine the butter, cinnamon, sugar and flour in a small bowl. Ladle the flour mixture on top of the fruit. Drizzle a little more flour on top of everything to cover any exposed fruit. Let cook for 15 minutes at 350 degrees F.

Nutrition Values:

Calories: 310 | Carbohydrates: 50g | Cholesterol: 31mg | Fat: 12g | Sodium: 5mg | Fiber: 5g | Protein: 2g | Sugar: 26g

STRAWBERRY LEMONADE VEGAN POP-TARTS

Preparation Time: 40 minutes | Cooking Time: 10 minutes | Servings: 12-14 pop tarts

Ingredients:

Pop-tarts

- ½ cup ice cold water
- ½ teaspoon vanilla extract
- 2 tablespoon light brown sugar
- 2/3 cup very cold coconut oil
- ¼ teaspoon salt
- 1 cup all-purpose flour
- 1 cup whole wheat pastry flour

Strawberry chia jam

- 3 tablespoon chia seeds
- 2 teaspoon maple syrup or as desired
- 2 tablespoon lemon juice or as desired
- 1 1/2 cups pitted dark cherries
- 1 1/2 cups sliced strawberries fresh or frozen

Lemon glaze

- ¼ teaspoon vanilla extract
- 2 tablespoon lemon juice
- 1 1/4 cup powdered sugar
- 1 teaspoon melted coconut oil
- Zest of 1 lemon
- Colorful sprinkles to garnish

Instructions:

Chia jam

1. Heat the strawberries and cherries in a saucepot until they begin to bubble and become syrupy. When super soft, mash with potato masher until the mix is jammy, loose and has some visible tiny bits of fruit.
2. Pour in the maple syrup and lemon juice. Taste and add more depending on the sweetness of the fruit.
3. Remove the mixture from heat and pour in a container. Add the chia seeds. Let the mix to set for at least 20 minutes or till it thickens up. You will have a lot of extra jam to use on oatmeal or toast throughout the week.

Pop-tarts

1. Combine sugar, salt, and flours in a large bowl. Chop in cold coconut oil with fork or pastry cutter until you get tiny-pea shaped pieces in dough.
2. Sprinkle in the vanilla and 1 tablespoon at a table. Pour in the ice cold water. The dough should be moist enough such that you can shape it into a ball without it flaking away and not sticky.
3. Divide the dough in half and then lightly flour your work surface and the rolling pin. Roll dough out to a few millimeters thick and slice into rectangles of 5 by 7 cm. Transfer the rectangles into a baking sheet that is lined with a parchment paper or silpat.
4. Put 1 heaping teaspoon jam on half of dough rectangles in the middle. Wet your finger and then moisten all around the perimeter. Place another rectangle on top and crimp the edges with fork to seal. Using a fork, make 3 sets of three holes into the top of pop tart. Continue with the remaining pop-tarts.
5. Heat your air fryer to 400 degrees F. Place 4 pop-tarts in the basket of air fryer and set time to ten minutes. Take out and repeat with remaining pop-tarts till all are cooked. Let to cool for approx. 20 minutes.

Lemon glaze

1. Combine the vanilla extract, coconut oil, lemon zest, lemon juice and powdered sugar in a bowl.
2. Spread around one teaspoon of icing onto each of pop-tarts and garnish with sprinkles and sugars you like. Let the icing to set and eat up!

Nutrition Values:

Calories: 272 | Carbohydrates: 36g | Fat: 14g | Saturated Fat: 11g | Sodium: 51mg | Fiber: 3g | Protein: 3g | Potassium: 125mg | Sugar: 18g

AIR FRYER CHOCOLATE CAKE

Preparation Time: 10 minutes | Cooking Time: 25 minutes | Servings: 4

Ingredients:

- 2 tsp vanilla
- 1/2 tsp baking soda
- 1 tsp baking powder
- 1/3 cup cocoa powder
- 1 stick butter, lukewarm
- 2/3 cup sugar
- 1 cup flour
- 1/2 cup sour cream
- 3 eggs

Instructions:

1. Preheat the air fryer to 320 degrees F.
2. Combine ingredients on low.
3. Place into oven attachment.
4. Put in the basket of air fryer and insert into air fryer.
5. Set the time to 25 minutes.
6. When time is done, poke the cake with a toothpick to check if done. If the cake doesn't spring back once touched, let cook for five more minutes.
7. Place the cake on wire rack to cool.
8. Then ice with your preferred chocolate frosting.

Nutrition Values:

Calories: 573 | Carbohydrates: 253g | Cholesterol: 861mg | Fat: 134g | Saturated Fat: 78g | Sodium: 962mg | Protein: 41g | Sugar: 139g

LEMON AIR FRYER POUND CAKE RECIPE

Preparation Time: 10 minutes | Cooking Time: 30 minutes | Servings: 4

Ingredients:

- Lemon juice - 1/4 cup
- Pure vanilla extract - 2 teaspoons
- Eggs - 2
- Lemon juice - 4 tablespoon
- Powdered sugar - 1 cup
- Sugar - 1 cup
- 1/2 cup 1 stick softened butter
- Salt - 1/4 teaspoon
- Baking powder - 1/2 teaspoon
- All-purpose flour - 3/4 cups

Instructions:

1. Preheat the air fryer to 330 degrees F.
2. Coat a six cup Bundt pan with grease and flour.
3. Combine together the salt, baking powder and flour in a bowl.
4. Place one cup of sugar and cream the butter in another bowl and combine well with your hand mixer. Keep the mixer running at low speed. Add 1 egg at a time and then add vanilla.
5. Alternating and combining after each addition, pour the dry mixture into butter mixture. Add ¼ cup of lemon juice.
6. Combine until smooth.
7. Transfer to the pan.
8. Bake for about 30 to 45 minutes until the middle has raised and a toothpick comes out dry when inserted into the middle.
9. In the meantime, prepare the glaze. Combine together four tablespoons of lemon juice, two tablespoons at time, and powdered sugar in a small bowl. Whisk in between adding lemon juice.
10. Let to cool for approx. 15 minutes and then flip out the cake on a plate.
11. Sprinkle on glaze using a spoon and cut. Serve.

Nutrition Values:

Calories: 273 | Carbohydrates: 37g | Cholesterol: 71mg | Saturated Fat: 7g | Sodium: 190mg | Protein: 2g | Sugar: 27g

PEACH HAND PIES IN AN AIR FRYER

Preparation Time: 15 minutes | Cooking Time: 12-14 minutes | Servings: 8

Ingredients:

- Cooking spray
- 1 (14.1-oz.) pkg. refrigerated piecrusts
- 1 tsp cornstarch
- 1/4 tsp table salt
- 1 tsp vanilla extract
- 3 tbsp. granulated sugar
- 1 tbsp. fresh lemon juice (from 1 lemon)
- 2 (5-oz.) fresh peaches (peeled and chopped)

Instructions:

1. In a medium bowl, combine together vanilla, salt, sugar, lemon juice and peaches. Allow to sit for 15 minutes while stirring often. Drain the peaches and reserve one tablespoon of liquid. Whisk the cornstarch into the reserved liquid and mix into the drained peaches.
2. Slice the piecrusts into eight circles of 4 inch. Put about one tablespoon of filling in the middle of each circle. Rub the edges of the dough with water. Fold the dough over the filling to make half-moons. Use a fork to crimp the edges and seal. Cut three small slits at the top of pies. Spray the pies well with cooking spray.
3. Transfer the pies to the basket of air fryer in a single layer. Let to cook for about 12 to 14 minutes at 350 degrees F. repeat this process with the remaining pies.

Nutrition Values:

Calories: 314 | Carbohydrates: 43g | Fat: 16g | Saturated Fat: 7g | Sodium: 347mg | Fiber: 1g | Protein: 3g | Sugar: 10g

AIR FRYER MASHED POTATO CAKES

Preparation Time: 40 minutes | Cooking Time: 6 minutes | Servings: 12

Ingredients:

- 2 cups panko crumbs
- 1 cup Flour
- 2 beaten eggs
- 1/2 teaspoon pepper
- 1 teaspoon salt
- 1/4 cup green diced onion
- 6-8 strips bacon (cooked and crumbled)
- 1 cup cheddar cheese, shredded
- 2 cups mashed potatoes

Instructions:

1. Fry your bacon till it's crispy. Then drain on paper towel until cool.
2. Crumble the bacon into small bits.
3. Transfer to a large bowl.
4. Add the green onions, cheddar cheese and mashed potatoes.
5. Mix to combine.
6. Line parchment paper onto a baking pan.
7. Transfer all the mashed mixture into the baking pan.
8. Evenly spread the potato mixture across the pan.
9. Transfer to your freezer for half an hour.
10. Using a circle cookie cutter, cut circles of the potato mixture and set aside
11. Continue cutting till you get all circles cut out.
12. Prepare the dredging station.
13. Add flour in one bowl, put eggs in the second bowl and place panko crumbs in the third bowl.
14. Dunk the potato cake in flour, then dip in eggs and lastly, dredge in crumbs.
15. Transfer the cakes to the air fryer.
16. Ensure to only cook in one layer of potato cakes in the machine.
17. Set temperature to 370 degrees F and cook for 6 to 8 minutes.
18. It's best when served right away while hot and crispy.

Nutrition Values:

Calories: 207 | Carbohydrates: 23g | Cholesterol: 44mg | Fat: 8g | Saturated Fat: 3g | Sodium: 419mg | Fiber: 1g | Protein: 7g | Potassium: 187mg | Sugar: 1g

AIR FRYER FRUIT PUDDING

Preparation Time: 10 minutes | Cooking Time: 25 minutes | Servings: 4

Ingredients:

Basic sponge pudding

- 1/2 teaspoon baking powder
- 2 oz. soft butter
- 2 tablespoon milk
- 1 egg
- 2 oz. sugar
- 3 oz. flour

Fillings

- 1 small can of pineapple or
- 2 large sliced peaches, or
- 4 large sliced plums

Instructions:

1. Combine the basic ingredients in bowl. Then beat well for three minutes until the mix is soft and creamy.
2. Stir in the filling ingredients or put in the base of a baking dish.
3. Transfer the pudding mixture into the dish and then smooth the level.
4. Cook in a preheated air fryer at 370 degrees F for about 25 to 30 minutes until turned golden.

Nutrition Values:

Calories: 319 | Carbohydrates: 47g | Cholesterol: 72mg | Fat: 13g | Saturated Fat: 7g | Sodium: 121mg | Protein: 5g | Potassium: 380mg | Sugar: 28g

VEGAN AIR FRYER CARROT CAKE FOR ONE

Preparation Time: 10 minutes | Cooking Time: 15 minutes | Servings: 1

Ingredients:

- 2 tsp of mild oil (or use applesauce or mashed banana to make oil-free)
- 1 tbsp. chopped dates or raisins
- 2 tbsp. chopped walnuts
- 2 tbsp. grated carrot
- 2 tsp unsweetened nondairy milk plus
- 2 tbsp. unsweetened nondairy milk
- Ground cloves, pinch
- Ground allspice, pinch
- 1/8 tsp ground dried ginger
- ¼ tsp ground cinnamon
- ¼ tsp baking powder
- 1 tbsp. coconut sugar or your preferred sweetener
- ¼ cup whole wheat pastry flour or use gluten-free baking mix

Instructions:

1. Grease an oven-safe mug with oil.
2. Add the salt, allspice, ginger, cinnamon, baking powder, sugar and flour.
3. Combine well with a fork. Be sure to mix well to distribute the baking powder evenly.
4. Add the oil, raisins, walnuts, carrot and milk. Combine once again.
5. Air fry for 15 minutes at 350 F. Insert a fork into the middle of the cake to check if done. If not done, cook for five more minutes.

Nutrition Values:

Calories: 421 | Carbohydrates: 52g| Fat: 22g | Sodium: 71mg | Protein: 8g | Potassium: 560mg | Sugar: 11g

Cooking Tip

You can make this cake extra special by combing one tablespoon vegan cream cheese and whip with one tablespoon powdered sugar to create a cream cheese topping.

AIR FRYER LEMON SLICE SUGAR COOKIES

Preparation Time: 15 minutes | Cooking Time: 10 minutes | Servings: 4

Ingredients:

- 1/4 tsp salt
- 1 tsp baking powder
- 1-1/2 cups all-purpose flour
- 2 tbsp. 2% milk
- 1 large egg, lukewarm
- 1/2 cup sugar
- 1 package (3.4 ounces) instant lemon pudding mix
- 1/2 cup softened unsalted butter,

ICING:

- 2 to 4 tsp lemon juice
- 2/3 cup confectioners' sugar

Instructions:

1. Cream sugar, pudding mix and butter in a large bowl for about 5 to 7 minutes until fluffy and light. Beat in milk and egg. Whisk salt, baking powder and salt in a separate bowl. Slowly beat into the creamed mixture.
2. Divide the dough in ½. Form each half into a six inch long roll on a lightly floured surface. Then wrap and place in the refrigerator for about three hours or until they're firm.
3. Preheat your air fryer to 325 degrees F. Unwrap the dough and slice crosswise into half inch slices. Working in batches, put the dough slices in a single layer onto a greased tray in the basket of air fryer. Let to cook for about 8 to 12 minutes until the edges become browned lightly. Allow to cool in the basket for two minutes. Transfer to the wire racks to cool completely.
4. Combine the confectioners' sugar and enough lemon juice to reach a drizzling consistency in a small bowl. Sprinkle atop the cookies. Allow to sit until set.
5. To prepare in advance: You can make the dough two days ahead. Wrap and put into a resealable container. The store in your refrigerator.
6. Freeze option: Put the wrapped logs into a resealable container and then place in a freezer. To use the frozen logs, unwrap them and chop into slices. Then cook as instructed and increase time by about 1 to 2 minutes.

Nutrition Values:

Calories: 110 | Carbohydrates: 17g | Cholesterol: 18mg | Fat: 4g | Saturated Fat: 2g | Sodium: 99mg | Protein: 1g | Sugar: 11g

CONCLUSION

Whether you have a small or large family or a small or large kitchen, there is an air fryer that will meet your expectations. You just need a reasonable amount of research to find the ideal air fryer that fits your cooking needs. Using the air fryer to cook your food is very easy even if you are a beginner. The recipes in this book are easy to prepare and the ingredients called for are easily available in your local grocery stores.

If you are a die-hard fan of fried foods and still would like to live a healthy life, you should consider air frying foods rather than deep-frying. This is because the air fryer reduces the amount of calories and fat and lowers the risk for development of dangerous compounds in food. Air frying will save you a lot of time in the kitchen especially if you are always on a tight schedule. You can even make a snack within ten minutes using an air fryer. Parents with school going kids can take advantage of this device to make a quick breakfast or meal without running late. Another benefit of air fryer is the ease of cleaning its parts. The parts are usually made of non-stick material and this prevents food particles from sticking on the surfaces. In addition, the basket, pan and grill are removable and dishwasher friendly.

I'd like to thank everyone who has read the contents of this book and I recommend every person to try out the fantastic recipes in the book. The recipes are easy to prepare and they are super delicious. Try them out to find out yourself! Remember to share with your friends and colleagues.